GETTING
IT
TOGETHER

Gaining
The Thriving
Professional's
Effective
EDGE

CHRISTINA RANDLE

Getting It Together

Gaining the Thriving Professional's
Effective *EDGE*

Second printing 2008
Printed in the United States of America
ISBN: 0-9788137-4-X

Credits
Design, art direction, and production   Melissa Monogue, Back Porch Creative, Plano, TX
    info@BackPorchCreative.com
Copy Editor   Kathleen Green, Positively Proofed, Plano, TX
    PositivelyProofed@sbcglobal.net

Endorsements

"Since adopting the lessons in this book I have been promoted twice, gotten more accomplished than I thought possible, and gained the balance in my personal life that we all strive for but rarely achieve."

Terry Taillard,
Division VP, **Frito Lay**

"This step-by-step, easy to follow formula made my productivity skyrocket and dramatically increased my effectiveness at work and in life."

Don Kendrick,
Regional President, **Wells Fargo**

"I recognized a number of my own faults and issues in the stories of Christina's clients. *Getting It Together* offered me a disciplined, supportive route to change that was easier than expected to accept and act on."

Tony Reilly,
Business Unit Director, **GP Worldwide**

"The Effective Edge gave me the tools to manage the ever present list of demands that normally define life. Instead, I now get to define them. Without The Effective Edge, I'd probably still be sitting in a cube somewhere responding to the news. With these ideas and methodology, I'm thriving."

Donald Broughton,
VP, **A.G. Edwards**

"This system has been life-changing for many employees who have participated. We have received consistently positive feedback about the system and the value the program provides in our e-mail-intensive world. Our teams have continued to reap the rewards for the long-term!"

MaryBeth Mongillo,
Learning & Development Manager, **Dell**

TABLE OF CONTENTS

INTRODUCTION

To survive: to stay alive; to continue to exist, subsist, endure.

To thrive: to grow vigorously: **FLOURISH***; to gain in wealth or possessions:* **PROSPER***; to progress toward or realize a goal despite or because of circumstances.*

– Merriam-Webster Dictionary

Recently, a consumer products company lost six senior executives in one 30-day period. When one of the remaining managers called me, he said he couldn't deal with his job and his work environment any more. The cost to his health and family – to their lives – is too much. No matter how much he accomplishes, it doesn't seem to be enough. He never turns off and, consequently, is mentally exhausted.

In fact, he – like the senior executives who moved on – has lost sight of the big picture and has lost his balance. As he struggles to put out internal fires, he finds less and less time to address strategic, forward-thinking and competitive issues. As a result, corrosion set in and began infiltrating every area of his life and business.

Rather than being ahead of the game, he was simply going through the motions. Instead of proactively planning and meeting long- and short-term objectives, he spent all of his time reacting.

Because he was always working – on his cell phone at his kid's soccer games, on his Blackberry during a rare dinner out and on the computer after his family had gone to bed – he'd lost sight of what really matters. He sacrificed everything for a paycheck, chasing the proverbial carrot on the stick and eventually, it was no longer enough.

Sound familiar?

Many of us are in the same boat. We're stressed out, overworked and overwhelmed because of the time we spend putting out fires, managing crises … and we are dog tired. As a result, our productivity suffers and we're anything but proactive.

We are caught up in the day-to-day tasks of our jobs and lives – running from meeting to meeting, checking e-mail, running errands, always feeling behind – and, bottom line, our lives are out of control. What's more, we've lost sight of our larger goals and passions. Balance seems totally out of reach, rather than something we can achieve – and enjoy.

Some of us are simply holding it together, wondering if we can really maintain the current pace over time. We may feel good about what we're doing, but we know we need to get better – and faster.

One of my favorite sayings is, "The better you get, the better you'd better get." If you're good at what you do, you don't get to rest on your laurels.

So how do we get it together? How can we *thrive* rather than simply survive?

Thriving is, in fact, a combination of art and science. The **art** is different for each of us and what it looks and feels like changes … as our environments and needs change. The **science** consists of implementing best practices, creating new and supportive habits and staying focused on the big picture.

But, thriving is tricky. It's like walking on a see-saw. Perfect balance involves constantly moving, not standing still until we fall off.

Here's an example: I was a single mom, just shy of my college degree, working a full-time professional job for a demanding boss. I was also a full-time student with not enough money to get by. As a result, I was always tired and conflicted about my priorities. There was little time for myself, and when there was, it seemed I chose things that further reduced my energy instead of rejuvenating it. Every day was a struggle – and I wondered how I would survive. It wasn't about my surroundings and circumstances, it was the way I was thinking and what I focused on. I didn't have a way to see the whole picture of my life and make good choices. It's at this point that I became a student of "effectiveness."

Today, my life is different. I thrive! I love what I do professionally and cherish having meaningful time with my family, friends and by myself, whether cycling, enjoying the quiet of nature or gardening. When my life is in balance, everything is easier. I'm in the zone more often and life flows effortlessly. I still have challenges and circumstances – those don't go away. But after learning and integrating the skills, habits and behaviors, I am now a Thriving Professional. I have the Thriving Professional's EDGE – the ability to manage my world effectively.

So, what can you do to move from merely surviving to thriving?

To become a Thriving Professional, I had to learn to organize, orchestrate and then execute on everything that was important to me ... everything, from work to family to "me" time. I also had to find ways to minimize the distractions that plagued my day, learn to say "no" and to set boundaries to protect what was important to me. I had to begin to recognize the signals for when I was surviving and those rare moments of thriving. I wanted more of the thriving!

This book has been written to provide you with the strategies, methodologies and tools I've found necessary to succeed as a Thriving Professional and the best practices in taking control of and managing your life in order to realize your dreams. I call it "The Effective EDGE." When I created it as a means of survival for myself, I began to thrive. I've refined it with over a decade of working with professionals like yourself.

The Effective EDGE is a combination of the way you think and make decisions about each new input of information you receive and how you move forward on everything that is important to you. The EDGE gives you tools to help you manage those decisions and your willingness to keep focused, change your behaviors when needed and get yourself energized around what you want to create for yourself – in all areas of your life. Simply stated, The Effective EDGE combines:

♦ **A Thought Process** – The Effective EDGE incorporates the best practices and proven strategies for making quick and effective decisions and taking action easily.

It's estimated that we make almost 750,000 decisions each year. Each decision provides a choice for us and changes the course of our lives. Most of those decisions, however, are work-related – the monotonous ones we have to make about e-mails, voice mails, when we will update the financial forecast for the meeting or make that call to check in with the person who called us last week. Are they effective? Do they enhance or take away our energy? We have about an 8- to 10-second window to decide. If we don't, we will usually forgo a decision and move on to the next things. We need to make decisions fast – and make them count – the big ones and the small ones.

♦ **A Tool** – Because of the number of these decisions and the fast pace of our lives, we need a practical tool to store those decisions so we can access them easily and at the right time. The EDGE uses a Personal Information Management (PIM) software program like Microsoft Outlook, Lotus Notes, GroupWise or any software that organizes your tasks and calendar. While some of us under utilize our tools, others are overusing advanced features that actually slow us down. The goal is to spend only the time necessary to prioritize tasks that will help us achieve a state of relaxed control. The tool allows us to keep everything in one location – and out of our heads so that we can better determine the best use of our time in every given moment.

♦ **Your Behavior** – You have to make a choice about how you want to work and live. We sometimes forget that. You can keep working the way you have been and get the same results or you can choose to make a change and try something different. We say, "If you keep on doing what you've always done, you'll keep on getting what you've always got!" While not grammatically correct, it sure rings true!

Try this to get an idea of what it feels like to change. Write your name as you normally do on a piece of paper or on the inside cover of this book. Now write it again – this time using your other hand.

How did it feel? Uncomfortable, slow, fun, exhilarating? Did you hesitate? Did you want to make it look perfect?

Welcome to change!

As with anything else, you can either choose change – or life will choose it for you. When YOU choose, you get to pick the timing of when your writing looks funny or takes more time to accomplish. When you don't make changes and wait until something or someone forces you to change, it is more difficult, more uncomfortable and more stressful to change.

Your willingness to examine and then change your behavior is the final element in gaining The Effective EDGE. If what you're doing now works 100 percent of the time, you wouldn't be reading this book. Maybe you are missing a small piece or maybe you need a total redo.

Whatever your reason, putting these three elements together can help you become a Thriving Professional. With The Effective EDGE, thousands of professionals from a variety of industries during the last decade have gained an hour and a half to two hours per day of increased productivity. They've also achieved:

- 23% increase in overall productivity.
- 17% improvement in delivering results on time.
- 15% decrease in work-related stress.
- 11% improvement in their ability to execute quickly.
- 98% decrease in time spent looking for things.
- 42% improvement in effectively prioritizing work.
- 29% increase in work/life balance.

Now, I invite you to journey through my story and those of several clients. By the end of this book, you, too, can be more productive, feel more successful, maintain balance and thrive!

CHAPTER 1

CHALLENGES AND CHOICES

The greatest glory in living lies not in never falling,
but in rising every time we fall.

– Ralph Waldo Emerson

We each confront a varying array of challenges. For some of us, these challenges may be managing workflow and staying organized. Others may find themselves blurring the boundaries between work and home. Still others don't know how to say "no" when "no" is definitely the best response.

Larry is founder and CEO of a 10-year-old, highly successful, mid-size technology company. He adores his wife, and his two girls are the sparkle in his eyes. Larry's always worked hard, is an avid reader, an active member of his church and loves his twice-a-week pick-up basketball game with friends. He could do without his visits with a personal trainer three times a week, but knows it's for his own good.

Larry called me because his business was expanding rapidly, but he was beginning to see some limitations in how he made decisions and managed himself. In short, he believed he was holding back his company.

During our first meeting, I asked Larry to describe a typical day.

"I'm pummeled with over 200 e-mails a day," he began, "and I can't focus on my work. My staff constantly interrupts me with minor emergencies and routine questions. I'm usually the first one to get here and the last one to leave, but I don't feel like I accomplish anything. All I do is move paper, check e-mails and react to interruptions, all day long. I don't feel proactive and, while my staff and board members rely on me to be the vision for this organization, I feel like I'm just reacting.

"I love this business," Larry admitted, "but I leave every day feeling frustrated and, quite honestly, I don't know how much longer I can do this."

In her mid-30s, Beth graduated with her MBA and worked her way up, starting in the training department of a state agency. She is now Senior Vice President of Organizational Effectiveness at a large investment bank. Quick-witted and with a ready smile, Beth loves to decorate, host parties and spend quiet evenings at home. Her greatest joy comes from assisting her internal customers, and she will go to any length to help. She's willing to put in the hours, but wants her hard work to pay off in more money and an increased title.

Beth is also frenetic and distracted. Working 11- to 12-hour days, she's sacrificing everything else for work. When I met Beth, the

Tasmanian Devil – the Warner Brothers cartoon character who tears around like a tornado, scaring everything in its path – came to mind. A fiery ball of energy, Beth's frenzied nature makes you want to stand back.

The long hours were what led her to me. She had been reprimanded by her boss for sending an e-mail to an internal client at 3 a.m. Her boss didn't care if she was working at that hour, but he didn't want anyone else to know. That's when she realized she needed to start doing things differently.

Although her office and desk were tidy, Beth was having trouble focusing during our first meeting. Jumping from topic to topic, she was easily distracted by unimportant things – like her new briefcase with wheels.

"I moved here about a year ago to take this position and don't really know anyone in the area," she began. "I work pretty long hours, but there is a lot to do, and I want to help the team. I bought a house and when I'm not at work, I spend time decorating it.

"At work, I have trouble finding things – things I know I've written down somewhere but can't put my hands on. I used to be so organized, but this group works on a wide variety of issues and I have to jump from topic to topic at the drop of the hat.

"I want to be a good team player," she continued, picking an unseen piece of lint from her neat black jacket, "but I seem to be taking on more projects than I can complete – that's another reason I work so many hours. I accept projects that aren't really my responsibility, but I don't want to say "no."

"I'm constantly thinking of things I need to do or projects we might want to take on. I just can't shut off my mind. I don't remember the last time I slept through the night."

She took a deep breath as she admitted, "My life doesn't seem to be going the way I planned. I was in Michigan when I decided to look for another job. I had wanted to return to Texas, but now I'm on the East Coast, and I don't even know how I got here."

Marcus is the plant manager for a major manufacturer. He's the father of twins and his wife is also a professional with a demanding job. Marcus' ideal weekend is to take his sons for a bike ride and then join his wife for lunch.

He doesn't have many hobbies, but loves his family time, although he doesn't have much. In fact, he cannot remember the last time he and his kids took that bike ride. Marcus isn't feeling very successful at work – or at home. He suspects his wife isn't that happy with him either, but he's afraid to even ask or think about that one.

He earned his first promotion after he'd been in his job for a few years. But now, he was afraid that if he didn't get it together, he might not make it in that job and with the company.

His office, a dark and dingy interior room in an old plant, is furnished with a metal desk and chairs. Papers are piled everywhere and boxes of supplies and equipment are stacked in every corner. Coiled maps and diagrams of processes lean against the wall.

There's no rhyme or reason to what's in his office. If there is a spot, there is something in it, even if he isn't responsible for it.

Marcus offered me a chair, then realized that all – except his own – had papers stacked in them. When I asked him to explain his situation, he collapsed in his chair, looking exhausted and overwhelmed. Truthfully, he looked ready to just give up.

"I've been really successful before and I want to make this work, but I'm not sure how to fix it. I was promoted to this position, inherited this office and had to hit the ground running, so I never had time to clean out the old stuff. The files I use are stacked on my desk, under the desk and on top of the credenza, but that's just the paper problem.

"From day one, I've felt like a human pinball. I manage from crisis to crisis, so there's never time to be proactive. I was in a meeting the other day with my boss and couldn't answer some of her basic questions about our performance, like the number of days without an accident or how many trucks we're getting off the lot each day. It was embarrassing.

"Because our plant operations are 24/7, I never get any down time. People call me at home at all hours. I'm so tired, I can't even think anymore, and I'm not sure my family remembers what I look like. I leave before the kids are up and get home after they've gone to bed, so I sometimes go days without seeing them. And I haven't been to a single school event this year."

Susan lives her passions! She is a plastic surgeon specializing in reconstructive surgery for cancer survivors. And her husband, a heart surgeon, was her sweetheart all through medical school and they love each other dearly. She has always wanted to be a physician and a mom – and she loves both roles, although she's begun to understand the challenges her family faces with both parents in high-stress positions. Now that she's achieved those goals, she struggles with how to manage everything – and still have any time for herself.

In addition to being a wife, the mother of two and a plastic surgeon, Susan also manages the surgical reconstruction center at a major hospital. Any of her roles would be a full-time job!

I was immediately struck by Susan's passion for her work and her family. Pictures of recovering patients, her husband and children shared the walls of her spotless office.

Her voice wavered with emotion as she confessed, "I love my life, but I am completely overwhelmed. I get tremendous satisfaction from my job – and my family is a gift beyond anything I could have imagined, but I just can't keep up with everything.

"I don't have anyone to turn to, no role models for how to do all of these things. Very few of the other doctors at the hospital take on these other roles. Most are not responsible for the household – the groceries, the cleaning or the family social calendar. And the family is fairly new to me. My husband and I have only been married for five years, our son is three and our daughter is under a year old."

"I feel I'm shortchanging everyone, and I don't want to give anyone – including myself – less than 100 percent. My unfinished To-Do's gnaw at me constantly and, intellectually, I know there's an easier way. I just don't know what it is or how to do it."

Do you identify with any of these people? Or are there parts of each story that resonate with you?

Are you bombarded by e-mail?

Are you drowning in paper?

Are you constantly interrupted by others?

Are you distracted and finding it difficult to focus on your work?

Are you sacrificing your health, family or friends for work?

What's the common thread running through each of these stories?

They all want more. They want not just to succeed, but to be Thriving Professionals. Each of them has become tired of just surviving, of being unfocused, unproductive and out of balance. They want full and productive careers as well as a balanced and satisfying life outside the office.

Are you – like Larry, Beth, Marcus, Susan – ready to learn how to get it together, to achieve The Effective EDGE? Are you ready to **thrive**?

CHAPTER 2

SEAMLESS & SIMPLE:
ELEMENTS OF THE EFFECTIVE EDGE

Work joyfully and peacefully, knowing that right thoughts and
right efforts will inevitably bring about right results.

– James Allen, American novelist

If you know anything about football, you know each team is made up of an offense and a defense. And it takes strength in both to win. A strong defense without a well-tuned offense won't score many points.

Unfortunately, many of us are playing defense at work. We're inundated by e-mails, phone calls, faxes and interruptions. E-mails and meetings drive our daily agenda and distract us from our key deliverables and objectives.

Like Larry, we feel bombarded. Spending each day reacting to whatever made its way into his world, Larry went from meeting to meeting, answering e-mails and phone calls in between. There was no time for his strategic work and no time to think or focus on the corporate vision.

And as Marcus walked around his plant, whatever problem he saw became an instant priority. Each new crisis pushed incomplete projects and tasks to the side. He found himself spending every day dealing with busy work rather than managing priorities and deliverables for the plant. The pace was frenetic.

Both Larry and Marcus needed to be able to capture their ideas – the To-Do's, their projects and everything they had promised themselves and others – into a system. They could track what they needed to accomplish and ensure timely completion of these tasks, from performance reviews or delivering the product to a client to making sure the new safety codes were being adhered to or buying their wife's anniversary gift. If they could track and complete tasks in a timely manner, they could be more productive and successful in all areas of their lives.

By keeping their eye on the big picture while performing their day-to-day tasks, Marcus and Larry needed to be sure that each task was headed in the right direction, seeing the end goal and the actions needed to get there. That's The Effective EDGE!

The Effective EDGE is a complete system for how a professional has to manage the whole of their lives – the big picture and the details, the calendars and To-Do's. Its approach and deciding model integrate all areas of your life – not just work. It is designed for the short- and long-term – personal and professional – and includes ways to handle and integrate all of the many pieces of information that we receive. That's some 225 new inputs daily! It gives you a way to make decisions quickly and effectively and put them into a place that you can trust now – and later. It also helps you design your life for how you want to live it – not just what you've been given.

This life-changing system is called The Effective EDGE and includes four main components.

The Effective EDGE™

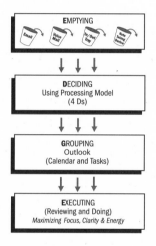

EMPTYING: We each have a number of places where we collect the things we need to do. When we put something in one of our collection points, we need to remember to go back and do something about it. If we have things stored everywhere, it's often frustrating just looking for a piece of paper or e-mail, trying to remember where we put it.

In The Effective EDGE, you identify all of your current collection points and then decide how many collection points are absolutely necessary. The goal is to narrow these collection points to four – or as close to four as possible.

A note of caution: Most of us use our e-mail inboxes as collection, storage and action points, which creates clutter, frustration and chaos.

Once your collection points are clearly defined, decide how frequently you need to empty them.

In my own system, I empty my e-mail inbox daily and my paper In tray weekly. As you use the system, you'll create your own process for emptying each collection point, regularly and frequently.

DECIDING: In The Effective EDGE, you use the EDGE Deciding Model™ to make effective and quick decisions on how to handle each piece of information instead of letting things pile up. You'll experience a 90 percent increase in productivity when you move decision-making to the front-end. How does this happen? Most of us "check our e-mail" or "take a look" at the pieces of paper that have arrived on our desk. We don't process, partly because we haven't learned how and partly because we feel like we don't have the time to really make a decision about that e-mail or piece of paper.

With The Effective EDGE, you will begin processing each new piece of information – no matter how it lands in your world. Rather than putting things aside or moving onto that unread e-mail, you will begin to confidently make decisions. It's easy, quick and painless. Think of the times you've opened an e-mail and closed it, only to come back to it later to open and close it again. Maybe you marked it unread or flagged it. As you went through these motions, no decision was made about that e-mail. Productivity and time are lost every time you review what you've already seen.

GROUPING: Sometimes lists can be overwhelming – either because of the length or the way the list is organized. Grouping allows you to put similar items together so that you can handle them quickly.

For instance, to find that list of agenda items for your boss, the phone calls you need to make or the errands that you need to run, you can skip the frustration and hassle by organizing your lists in a PIM software program that helps you manage what you need to do and track the tasks you've delegated.

EXECUTING: Most of us want to spend more time accomplishing goals and moving things forward. In order to do this, we need to ensure that we have a seamless system, delivering on all that we promised and moving the right things forward at the right time, rather than just checking e-mail, trying to remember what we've promised. By creating and maintaining The Effective EDGE, you can move through the first three components quickly, spending more time executing.

The Effective EDGE also includes the best practices that enable you to stay focused, relaxed and confident. You will learn how to begin your day, rejuvenate and refocus yourself with the Weekly Recharge and create powerful and energizing Intentions.

The Effective EDGE helps you clear the clutter, organize tasks in all areas of your life and focus on the right things at the right time. In doing so, it allows you to be proactive and creative, making room for new ideas. Ultimately, you emerge with relaxed control, confident in knowing what you need to do because you have The EDGE.

The key experiences resulting from using The Effective EDGE in your life can be summarized by the five concepts below:

MIND LIKE WATER

As you implement The Effective EDGE, you want to achieve a state of "Mind Like Water," a martial arts concept that illustrates why clarity is so important. Think of a calm, still pond. When you throw a pebble into the water, the pond ripples in direct proportion to the size of the pebble. Throw in a larger rock and the pond responds with a larger ripple before returning to a calm and still state. However, if the water is choppy and you throw in a pebble, the pond's response won't be proportionate.

Your mind is much like that pond. When your head is clear, you can respond appropriately to all the things life throws your way. When your mind is choppy – filled with the buzz of ideas and the effort required to manage your day in your head – you either over-react or under-react to each new task that emerges.

The Effective EDGE gives you a place to store the things that are on your mind – from the tasks of a budget that needs updating to the article you need to read to a reminder to pick up your dry cleaning. When you use The Effective EDGE to clear your head of the issues and tasks that distract you, you can focus on the new opportunities and creative ideas.

FOCUS VS. MULTITASKING

In the real estate industry, one often-repeated mantra is, "Location, location, location." If you're becoming a Thriving Professional, your mantra is, "Focus, focus, focus!"

It takes 2-4 minutes to fully focus – to get into the zone – and a split second to move out of it.

Many of us spend our days being pulled in many different directions, often at one time. We find ourselves trying to accomplish multiple tasks, thinking this is the only way we can get through the day.

Honestly, how often do you try to answer your e-mail while you are on a conference call, returning voice mails or talking to someone?

When we attempt to focus on two things at one time, we are multitasking. However, there is a cost. When we focus fully on one thing, we are giving 100 percent and getting the best result we can. However, if we separate that same amount of focusing energy between two things, it reduces the amount of energy we have for each item to 40 percent. How? Twenty percent of our energy is spent just going back and forth between the two items. That leaves 40 percent for each. Anything less than 50 percent and we frequently don't remember something or don't trust the decision that we made. Our choice – 100 percent or 40 percent. You have to decide if you can afford a 40 percent decision!

Studies show that multitasking is not only counterproductive because it takes longer to complete each individual task, but that it can actually lower your IQ. Dr. Glenn Wilson, a psychiatrist at King's College London University, studied the work styles of 80 professionals and found the IQ of people who tried to multitask fell by 10 points throughout the day – the equivalent to missing a whole night's sleep and more than double the four-point fall seen after smoking marijuana.

Said Dr. Wilson during a CNN interview, "This is a very real and widespread phenomenon. We have found that this obsession with looking at messages, if unchecked, will damage a worker's performance by reducing their mental sharpness."

The Effective EDGE gives you a time and place to deal with all the new messages or paper coming into your world while helping you focus on the work in front of you. As you implement The EDGE, give yourself permission to focus rather than multitask.

The choice is yours. Can you afford 40 percent?

BIG VS. SMALL: MOTIVATING VS. MANAGING

With issues and tasks bombarding us every day, it's easy to get lost in the details and minutiae. So a key to thriving is keeping the big picture in focus while being confident you are performing the right steps to accomplish each goal. But how?

A typical To-Do list has all sorts of information on it. Some items are small — schedule a meeting or pick up dry cleaning. Some items are big — implement Sarbanes-Oxley regulations and ensure full compliance or sell current house and buy another one. It also includes everything in between — all on one list.

Needless to say, it's easy to get lost, confused or frustrated as we move from item to item. Why? Because there are so many different kinds of things on our lists, including items we've overlooked or simply left there because we have no time to complete them.

With The Effective EDGE, your lists are simplified. First, put all the big items together, for instance, all of your projects. Knowing that you have eight projects in progress and their due dates makes it simple.

Here's another suggestion that will simplify your life: We often put items from our personal development plan in a file folder in the credenza, our personal goals in a file at home and our business goals on the white board next to the door in our office. In other words, they're all over the place. By putting them all in the same place — on ONE list, you can now see how they all come together.

Why does this consolidation work? It streamlines our focus, brings clarity and ensures that we match the right level of effort to each project. At the same time, we're moving all areas of our life forward.

By consolidating tasks and goals, you'll be clear on what you are focusing on *and* what you aren't focusing on. What we focus on, we get more of – but we need it in front of us to make sure we focus on it.

One more thing about focus: You've got to focus on the big things to make sure all of the small things go in the right direction. But, here's the catch: Sometimes our small things aren't small enough.

KEEPING OUR TO-DO'S SMALL AND MOVING

We love crossing things off our lists. It makes us feel really good. We have the sense that we are making progress. At one time or another, some of us have even completed something and then written it down just to be able to cross it off! When we cross things off, it gives us a sense of satisfaction and best of all, it gives us more energy.

Some of our To-Do lists have items on them that we aren't getting done. Too many "incompletes" reduce our energy and make us feel overwhelmed because we aren't making progress. After looking at many To-Do lists over the last decade, I've noticed that the common thread for the items not getting done is that the items are too big and need to be broken down even more – or at least written with more clarity.

Most of us are so busy, when we look at an item on our list and can't figure out **exactly** what we need to do, we have a tendency to move on to the next item. The item we skipped just sits there.

Using The Effective EDGE, we use statements, written clearly, to make it easier to understand what we need to accomplish. Here's an example: "Payroll Report." If this was on your list, would you know what to do? Probably not. How about this: "Call Marty about exceptions on Q3 payroll report." Now, do you know exactly what's required?

If our lives moved slower, our networks were smaller and we received less decision-demanding information each day, then writing only "Payroll Report" might work. For most of us, however, that's just not reality. We have to write down tasks, using specifics, to know exactly what to do – even if we look at it a few days or a week later.

NOW VS. SOMEDAY/MAYBE – OUR ABILITY TO COMMIT

When we think of something we need to do, many of us write it down and try to make it happen. As we write, we often don't think about whether it's the right time or if we have what we need to make it happen.

Now, here's the problem: You may not have the time, the energy or the resources to take care of it now. So, what happens? The item languishes on your list, getting skipped over. Yet, there's a part of you that feels you should be getting it done – because it's on your list.

In The Effective EDGE, you create a place to store those items – a place called a "Someday/Maybe list." That's not to be confused with procrastination or actions you cannot do right this minute. These are things that should not be put on your list right now because you can't commit to them.

Whenever you think of tasks you need or want to do, ask this critical question to determine if you have what's needed to make that idea happen: "Do I have the time, money, energy and resources to make this happen – now?"

For instance, one of my clients just shared a great idea that I would like to try at our next quarterly team meeting. Because we just had a team meeting a few days ago, it's too early to be thinking about next quarter, so I add the suggestion to my Someday/Maybe list so that it can incubate.

Sometimes we have ideas about what we'd like to do, but don't have the personnel to make it happen. Or, a friend brings great pictures of his vacation and we'd really like to go. But now is not the time to begin thinking about that next vacation.

We all need an idea or Someday/Maybe list, a place to allow our creativity to continue and even expand. This list should be a place where ideas percolate. When we decide to move an item to our Someday/Maybe list, it frees up energy that we can then put toward items that can and should happen now.

As you're probably noticing, using The Effective EDGE to make simple changes in how you approach your day is part of becoming a Thriving Professional. You'll focus on the right things at the right time, multitask less, move projects forward and deliver on your goals, both personal and professional. You'll also be able to deliver on previous promises and handle all of the new items and information coming into your world.

What is the way out of just surviving? EDGE your way out by **Emptying, Deciding, Grouping and Executing!**

CHAPTER 3

MIND LIKE WATER:

THE KNACK OF EMPTYING

A ruffled mind makes a restless pillow.

– Charlotte Bronte

The first step in The Effective EDGE is to collect all of the information you receive and things you need to do in one of four pre-defined collection points. Until now, you may have collected things in numerous places. The obvious ones are your e-mail boxes, cell phones, office voice mail, your In tray, if we have one, stacks on your desk, tablets (sometimes even multiple ones going simultaneously), your briefcase, wallet, and white boards. Some of us even have more creative places like stacks under our desk, the back seat of our car, bottom of our purse, a drawer in our credenza, a bulletin board or under magnets on our refrigerator. We collect in lots of places.

You may think you've dealt with the item because you've stored it somewhere out of sight, but if you can't quickly act on it, you don't really have a system – just places to put things … and probably too many places, at that.

Remember those stacks of papers in Marcus' office – in every chair, on the desk, under the desk, on top of the file cabinets? When he returned from an out-of-town conference, he was surprised to find yellow crime scene tape wrapping his office. Although his co-workers thought it pretty funny, the cluttered office where Marcus worked, or tried to, made it difficult for him to focus and move the right projects forward. How could he determine what required action as opposed to what just needed to be filed or – even better – thrown away?

Marcus was paralyzed by his clutter, unable to focus. He spent as little time at his desk as possible because it was an uncomfortable place to be. And who could blame him? He inherited a full office from his predecessor and, rather than taking the time to sort through, throw out and get a handle on things, he started storing his own work wherever he could find an empty space. The next thing he knew, it felt so small – as if he was working in a storage closet instead of a workspace.

Larry's e-mail inbox was overflowing. He "checked" it several times each day, but left messages in the inbox, even after he was finished with them. With so many e-mails, he couldn't tell which needed action, which could be filed and which could be deleted.

Beth had so many thoughts and ideas and To-Do's floating around in her head, she woke herself up during the night. She seldom got any quality sleep because she seemed to always be worrying about the things she had to do. Even during the day, she kept interrupting herself with her own thoughts.

Having too many places where you collect things creates chaos.
You had that piece of paper or e-mail yesterday, but now you don't
know where you put it. When someone asks you for information,
you have to search for it, even though you're certain you just had it
in your hand or were just looking at it – was it yesterday or maybe
the day before?

The top of the following diagram illustrates some of the many
places you might be collecting information. Where else are you
collecting your To-Do's? Do you have To-Do's written on Post-it®
notes, stuck around your workspace? Scan your environment. Is
the project you need to work on at the office sitting on your desk
at home? What about your head?

The Effective EDGE™

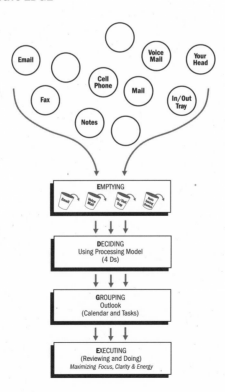

With The Effective EDGE, you pare your multiple collection points down to four buckets – your e-mail inbox, voice mail, an In/Out tray for paper and a note-taking device. Think of these buckets as trash cans – you collect there and then empty them regularly, never letting any of them get so full that they overflow.

E-mail Inbox: Use your e-mail inbox to collect **new** electronic messages. The inbox isn't designed for long-term storage or for organizing To-Do's. To put it simply: Don't try to manage your work in your e-mail inbox.

Do you get "nastygrams" from your IT department when your mailbox is over its size limit? That's a sure sign you're abusing it.

Start using the e-mail inbox to collect new information today. Then, process and empty it each day.

Some of us live in e-mail. We wait for each new e-mail to arrive and then check it. If we get 100 e-mails a day, that means we are checking e-mail that often. The problem is, studies tell us the more time we spend in e-mail, the less effective we are. We need more focus time. Hanging out in our e-mail inbox doesn't give us that focus time.

We'll show you in the Executing chapter a proven method to handle all of those incoming e-mails. Spend less time there! But more about that later.

Voice Mail: Your voice mail inbox is for collecting phone messages. You may have several voice mail boxes – home, work and cell.

In/Out Trays: The In/Out trays sitting on top of your desk or credenza are for collecting paper. They're labeled "In" and "Out" so people know where to leave paper for you. It's also a great place to collect notes and materials you pick up from meetings that you attend. Using an In tray as the collection point keeps your entire office from being your inbox!

New paper information is collected in your In tray. When you have completed a task, you can place it in your Out tray until it is time to deliver the item.

Here's another idea for In/Out trays that works at home: My husband and I each have our own set of trays. Instead of leaving mail for each other lying around, we each have one dedicated place – rather than all over the house.

Note-Taking Device: Whatever did you do with those quotes you need for that report you're working on? Did you put it on a sticky note, the back of a memo or did you jot it on a scrap of paper that's lost in your briefcase?

If you're tired of spending time searching for the notes you made – on the phone, in your car … on a sticky note, a note pad, or the back of a meeting agenda – a note-taking device will change your life forever. All of those important notes can now be found in one place!

Most find a spiral-bound 5x7 notebook the best – and least expensive. This note-taking device serves as a single place where you can take notes in a meeting, write down random thoughts, record phone conversations, record voice mail and take notes related to projects that you are working on. It's nice if it has a small pocket as well as perforated pages so that they can be removed without ripping. You can get a good clean page to start new topics. It needs to be nice enough and portable so that you will take it anywhere! We collect information everywhere we go – even if it's a reminder to call that client who just randomly pops into our heads. Therefore, we need to have a place to collect information anywhere we are!

Empty these four collection points regularly. Most e-mail boxes need to be emptied daily as these items are more urgent in nature than the paper In tray or our Notes. As you empty each one, use The EDGE Deciding Model™ (described in Chapter 4) to determine what to do with each piece of new information. Then, group it in the appropriate location in your PIM software. It's only when you can see all of your To-Do's in one place that you can prioritize and get the right things done at the right time.

Your goal is to get to the **Executing** step as quickly as possible. Why? Because that's where you are measured. Think back to your performance plan. It probably doesn't include kudos and incentives for collecting thousands of e-mails in your inbox, but is based, instead, on how much work you accomplish and how many projects you complete.

So, how do you get to "Executing?" By streamlining your collection points, making good, quick and solid decisions on the information collected – e-mail, phone and paper – and simplifying your lists so that you can quickly move on things at the right time.

YOUR HEAD IS NOT A COLLECTION POINT
Did you notice that your head didn't make the cut as one of the four collection buckets? This is because your head is not a reliable storage device. It is difficult for us to focus if we are trying to

manage all the information that we receive in our heads. Pardon the pun, but this is a no-brainer!

Many of us make about 750,000 decisions each year. Most of these decisions are related to work, e-mails, voice mails and calls that infiltrate our workspace. Once they arrive, it's up to us to decide what to do with them.

Like Larry and Marcus, we can try to manage all of those decisions in our heads, but our brains are best used for problem-solving, creative ideas and processing information – not storage facilities. If we use our brain power for less meaningful tasks, like cataloging our To-Do lists, we're guilty of squandering our precious intellectual capital.

Have you ever had this happen? You think of something really important that you want to do that day. You dress for work, have breakfast, drop the kids off, check your voice mail on the way to work, get to work and are stopped by someone in the hallway. You finally get to your office, just in time to check your e-mail and run to a meeting.

The entire day continues at this pace. On the way home, you finish up those last calls, pick up something for dinner, have dinner and then crash in front of the TV.

As you begin to relax, you're suddenly engulfed with a sense that you've forgotten something. What is it? (Hear the theme from the movie "Jaws" playing in the background? "Da-dum, da-dum, da-dum.") Then it dawns on you. It's that one thing – that one item you absolutely needed to accomplish. You reminded yourself of it first thing this morning. It had to be done ... and it wasn't!

Want to stop this "buzz" in your head – this sense of discomfort and anxiety?

Write it down immediately! Place each new To-Do in one of your four collection points. This ensures you'll remember what needs to be done and gets rid of that gnawing anxiety that you are going to forget something important.

Here's something to consider: You can only hold 3-7 items in your conscious mind at one time. When something new moves into your head, something old drops into your unconscious mind. You don't forget it. It's just no longer top-of-mind. You've gone unconscious about that item.

When do you remember that To-Do? At three o'clock in the morning when you are trying to sleep, your head is clear and you aren't thinking about anything else. You have some room now in your conscious mind so your brain is basically asking, "Can you handle this thing now?" If you don't write it down then, it will continue to come back – again and again – until you have it written down. Why waste all that time? Why create all that stress for yourself??

CLEARING YOUR HEAD

You are attending a presentation, and rather than listening to the presenter, you find yourself thinking of all the things you need to do.

It's the weekend and you're all set to relax, to get some exercise or complete that garden project you've wanted to do all year. Instead of enjoying the weekend, though, you're paralyzed by a head filled beyond capacity with work tasks and other things.

You feel overwhelmed by things you need to do and you even wake up at night, thinking about what's happening at work next week.

These are signs you need to clear your head. So, here's how.

Stay with me here: During World War II and continuing even today, the U.S. Navy operates ships called "mine sweepers." The most important job of these vessels is to, literally, "sweep" clean the sea lanes – particularly harbors used by the U.S. – of mines and other enemy explosives.

With The Effective EDGE, we recommend something called "the Mind Sweep" to clear your head of all of the To-Do's and record them in your PIM software. We want to get them out of our head before they blow up!

As you create your list, don't try to separate the personal from the professional. Trying to maintain two separate lists isn't easy in today's warp-speed world, plus the lines between our personal and professional lives break down pretty fast.

Make it easy on yourself. ONE person, ONE life, ONE list!

TRY IT: Mind Sweep Exercise

1. Open your PIM software.

2. View the task or To Do section where you can type in the list of To-Do's.

3. Enter each of your To-Do's in its own record – creating a new task for each item. Put both personal and professional

items on the list – one life, one list. Some personal things have to be taken care of during business hours and some professional things can only be done on weekends, so it is better to have everything you need to take care of in one place in order to evaluate how much you have to do.

4. Take 10-15 minutes to really clear out your head.

How do you feel? Isn't it great to have all of that "stuff" out of your head?

There aren't many times in life when someone will encourage you to have an "empty" head, but keeping your head empty of information that can be captured elsewhere provides tremendous relief. You'll be able to focus on what's at hand without fear of forgetting that one thing you're trying to remember.

CAPTURE YOUR TASKS, RECLAIM YOUR ENERGY

In addition to becoming overwhelmed, not recording your incomplete tasks also drains your energy and causes you to feel worn out by the end of the day.

Have you ever left the office, completely sapped of energy as you drag yourself to your car? To recapture your energy, you not only have to capture your incomplete tasks, but also acknowledge the work you've finished.

There is a cycle of energy with each task that begins when you receive any new information that requires your decision and/or action. You think: "I need to do something with that, but I'll deal with it later," which causes your energy to begin to decline.

Once you begin taking action, your energy starts to ramp back up. When you finish the task, your energy cycles up even further, but you don't completely regain your initial energy until you take the time to acknowledge the task's completion.

Have you ever marked a task off your To-Do list? Didn't it feel great?

People mark things off their list because it's energizing. But, in order to cross off your completed items, you first have to record them somewhere.

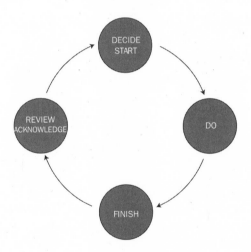

All the uncaptured, incomplete items and information spinning around in your head zap your stamina and cause your focus to blur. Your energy decreases in direct proportion to the incomplete items in this cycle and increases as you complete tasks or move them toward completion.

To recapture your energy completely, capture your To-Do's on your task list and acknowledge your accomplishments, no matter how small. The more items checked off, the more energy you'll have!

Larry faced this challenge. While he was accomplishing a great number of things during the day, he didn't feel he was making any progress toward his goals. As he implemented The Effective EDGE, he started capturing his tasks in his PIM software and marking them, "Complete." Taking time to acknowledge his accomplishments and cross them off his list gave him the satisfaction he had been lacking and allowed him to end each day feeling more energized. Why? Because he knew he had moved forward on his goals.

You've just completed the first step to becoming a Thriving Professional with The Effective EDGE – **"Emptying."** You've minimized your collection points and cleared your head of all the tasks you need to do. Now, it's time to make decisions about how to handle each of those items.

CHAPTER 4

10-SECOND DECISIONS:

DECIDING WITH THE EDGE

4 QUESTIONS & 4 CHOICES – EASY & FAST

It is only in our decisions that we are important.

– Jean-Paul Sartre

You've narrowed your information collection points to four and you've learned now to check and empty these regularly.

Logically, the next step is to make a decision about this new data that constantly makes its way into your world.

If you're like most of us, it's pretty common to open and scan an e-mail and then close it and move on to the next one. Or maybe you pick up a piece of paper, peruse it and put it aside saying you'll deal with it later when you have time. The next thing you know, you have a full e-mail inbox and stacks of paper on your desk you're not sure what to do with. And, as often happens, you can become immobilized by indecision. Postponing decisions can turn us from a "handle-it-when-it-shows-up manager" to a "handle-it-when-it-blows-up manager."

To become a Thriving Professional, your next task is to learn to make decisions quickly about how to handle each item, whether taking action or deferring it to the future. Each decision should only take about 10 seconds to make.

Businesses operate using systems. If you want to make decisions you can trust, you need to use the same process each time. The EDGE Deciding Model™ helps you handle each new item in just a few seconds.

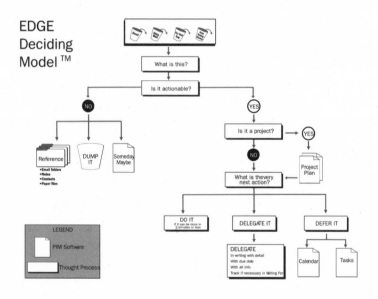

To get started, ask the following critical decision-making questions for each new piece of information you receive:

Question 1. "What is this?" – Focus your attention, solely, on the item in front of you. Focusing allows us to make decisions that we count on now – and trust later. Remember, it's either 100 percent or 40 percent. Can you afford 40 percent?

Question 2. "Is it actionable?" – Analyze whether this item requires action. For most of us, 50 percent of the information we receive is not actionable and can be quickly discarded, filed or added to our Someday/Maybe list.

The key to the "Is it actionable?" question is to clear non-actionable items out of the way. That's right; throw them out, file them or incubate them now so that you can focus on the things that do require action. If the item is actionable, move on to the next question.

Question 3. "Is it a project?" – Determine whether the task has more than five steps, which would classify it as a project. A task with five steps or more is one of your big-picture items. Projects require more thought and planning than just placing an action item on a list. They represent significant deliverables and are often strategic in nature. (You'll learn how to design an effective project in Chapter 7.)

Question 4. "What's the very next *ACTION*?" – This allows you to plan the very next step you need to take. Called "your next action," this step is different than making a To-Do list. Why? Because To-Do lists are often a combination of big and small things, strategic and non-strategic items, specific or vague items. To-Do list items also frequently have dependencies, meaning the item listed can't be completed until something else happens first.

Here are a few more tips:

♦ Make your *ACTION* list clear and concise, containing the next independent action that can be done in one sitting. A good example is having an item like "budget report" on your To-Do list. That item could mean a number of things like draft the report, recalculate some fields in the report, or approve it.

♦ If you're staring at a task, trying to figure out what to do, or if you keep skipping over it, it might be too vague or it could need to be broken into smaller steps.

♦ To-Do's often have dependencies. *ACTIONS* do not. *ACTIONS* are specific and independent. Manage by *ACTIONS* using the tasks and the calendar features in your PIM software.

As you write each of your tasks, use the *ACTIONS* criteria:

Action verb at the beginning – such as call, e-mail, review or write.

Can you see yourself doing it? If you can't, you'll skip it.

Thought Process – Use the EDGE Deciding Model™ to determine the required *ACTION*.

Independent. Requires no other steps before you perform this *ACTION*.

One sitting to complete – whether 15 minutes or one hour.

Next strategic step. Until this *ACTION* is performed, no other step can be taken.

Specifics are required. You know exactly what needs to be done.

The following illustrates the difference between a traditional To-Do and an *ACTION*:

Examples of To-Do's:	**Examples of *ACTIONS*:**
• Training for AT&T	• E-mail Fred re: training deadline
• Clean garage	• Pack boxes
• Weekly report	• Talk to Joanne re: report format

Ready to try it? Here are a few more helpful hints:

♦ Be specific enough that someone else could look at your list and determine generally what needs to be done.

♦ Test each *ACTION* for the 8- to 10-second scan. If it takes more than 8-10 seconds to figure out what to do, you will skip over it.

♦ Are there things on your task list that are past due? Maybe you could not see yourself doing them because they felt too big or had too many dependencies.

♦ Break down the To-Do's into small steps that can be accomplished with ease. Remember the saying: "It's a cinch by the inch but it's hard by the yard."

Once you have identified the very next *ACTION*, it's time to decide how and when to act on it.

From here, you have three more questions...

♦ **"Can I do it in two minutes or less?"** If an *ACTION* can be done in two minutes or less, then Do It! Get it off your plate now. About 30 percent of the items you receive each day can be handled in two minutes or less. With a small task, it can take more time to defer it than to just do it! Create a mindset of taking care of things quickly when possible.

♦ **"Can I delegate it?"** Can't handle in two minutes or less? Delegation is ensuring that the right person is doing the right level of task, whether it is asking a boss or peer or a staff member to take on a task. Consider whether you really are the best person to handle it. If not, delegate those items and clear them out so you can focus on the work you need to get done.

As you delegate, do it in writing – with sufficient detail so the recipient is clear on what needs to be done and how you want it handled. Delegating in writing helps you communicate clearly and thoroughly. Include due dates and specifics about resources needed to complete the task. Track the delegated item on your task list so you will remain accountable for the work to be done.

♦ **Do I need to defer it?** If an *ACTION* requires more than two minutes to perform and can't be delegated to someone else, defer it to your calendar or task list so that it can be done later. No, this isn't procrastination. It's you making a decision. However, because the *ACTION* takes more than two minutes, you will delay taking the action until after you complete the processing of your inbox.

But, once you defer the *ACTION*, where does it go?

Two types of *ACTIONS* go on your calendar and two belong on your task list. But, before you decide where it goes, look for four keywords associated with the acceptance of a new *ACTION*. It either needs to be done **AT** a certain time, **ON** a certain date, **BY** a certain date or doesn't have a due date (**NO**).

These keywords help you determine whether to put the *ACTION* on the calendar or the task list.

WHAT GOES ON YOUR DAILY CALENDAR?

♦ *ACTIONS* that occur **AT** a specific time. Most programs refer to these as appointments, i.e., meet with John **AT** 1 p.m. Tuesday to review new operations manual.

♦ *ACTIONS* that occur **ON** a specific day, but not at a specific time, i.e., "Talk with John **ON** Monday to review new operations manual." Most PIM programs refer to these calendar items as All Day Events since they are not time specific. Use these All Day Events to store birthdays and anniversaries as well as *ACTIONS* you need to do on a specific day but not at any particular time.

You currently may be forcing these *ACTIONS* into a time slot on your calendar, even though they don't have to be done at that time. For example, you need to call John on Monday and put the call at 3 p.m. on your calendar, even though it could be handled anytime that day. Instead, use your calendar to assign No Time or All Day Event to list these *ACTIONS* on that day without a time slot.

Word of Caution: You don't want to dilute your calendar with *ACTIONS* that aren't time-specific. Don't assign times or dates unless the *ACTION* must really be performed on that date. Why? Because you know the time isn't real so when you get pulled into another project, you skip that *ACTION*. Keep your calendar "honest" by only putting things in the time slots that really belong there.

WHAT GOES ON THE TASK LIST?

♦ *ACTIONS* or Projects to be done **BY** a specific date, i.e., "Review operations manual with John **BY** April 30."

This is different than the **ON** keyword because these *ACTIONS* could be completed anytime before the due date, but must be delivered **BY** that date. For example, we can file our taxes anytime before April 15, but they must be submitted BY the 15th.

♦ *ACTIONS* or Projects that have **NO** due date, i.e., "Review the operations manual with John."

Tasks with no due date make up the largest percentage of our *ACTIONS*. Don't make up a due date if there isn't a real due date. Add it to your list with **NO** date. Don't worry. It will still get taken care of !

The Effective EDGE uses REAL information when establishing due dates to reflect the true realities of what you've agreed to do. Making up due dates doesn't work.

If maintaining privacy is a concern, many PIM software applications give you the capability to mark personal appointments or tasks as "private" so others viewing your calendar cannot see the details of these appointments or tasks.

TRY IT: Processing your Collection Points

It's time to apply The EDGE Deciding Model.™ If you haven't already, gather all of your loose paper (from your desk, briefcase or other hiding places) and put it in your In tray. Empty your voice mail and grab your note-taking device so you can review your notes. Process each of these collection points using the following steps:

1. Handling one item at a time (piece of paper, voice mail message, e-mail, etc.), use The EDGE Deciding Model™ to decide what to do.

2. If you defer the item, enter it either as a calendar or task item in your PIM software.

3. Open your e-mail inbox. Process each message stored in the inbox, using the flowchart on page 19. You might find it helpful to use a shortcut, called the 4 D's, for remembering the choices in the model. Look at the model and notice that there are four actions that start with the letter D:

   • Dump It (or file it)

   • Do It (if it can be done in 2 minutes or less)

   • Delegate It

   • Defer It

Use the 4D's to quickly empty your e-mail inbox several times each day.

At first, it may feel overwhelming to have a long task list in your personal organizer. But you already had these tasks, they just weren't in one place. Now you can be confident knowing where everything you need to do is stored and that you can stay on top of it.

Decide to be a Thriving Professional!

CHAPTER 5

GROUPING YOUR ACTIONS:

MAKING YOUR LIST MAKE SENSE

*Crude classifications and false generalizations
are the curse of organized life.*

– George Bernard Shaw

Long before someone came up with the idea of plastic divider trays for silverware, all the knives, forks and spoons were simply washed, dried and dumped into a drawer after every meal. When it came time to set the table for the next family meal, someone had to search through the scrambled pile of silverware to find enough utensils. Eventually, all the necessary silverware was found. It just took time.

A traditional To-Do list is much the same. There's no rhyme or reason to it. Each item – big or small – is listed after the next, and tasks aren't categorized or organized.

To provide order and focus to your task list, create categories or keywords to group similar kinds of *ACTIONS* together, streamline your focus and effectively prioritize what you need to do next. This will help you determine what you need to do, and when you need to do it.

The following 11 categories were developed from my work with professionals for more than a decade. The dots before each category or code name ensure that the list sorts based on its priority in the hierarchy of your list.

◆ The ... (triple dot) category represents your big-picture items: Projects (which we will discuss in detail in Chapter 7) and ...Intentions (which we will discuss in detail in Chapter 8).

◆ The .. (double dot) categories are the items you look at every day: Your *ACTIONS*, items you need to discuss with your manager or team and items you have delegated.

◆ The . (single dot) categories are *ACTIONS* you don't look at as often.

This dot hierarchy was developed for PIM software that sorts items with more dots to the top of the list. If your PIM software sorts items with more dots lower on the list, then you need to modify the category names so that Projects is a single-dot category (.Projects) and categories like Errands and Home are triple-dot categories (...Errands or ...Home).

...INTENTIONS. This category is your overarching, long-term personal and professional category. These are the dreams you are pursuing, the organizational initiatives you have a part in rolling out, etc.

...PROJECTS. In this category, you store the name, description and outcome of the projects to which you have committed. Remember: Projects are tasks that require more than five steps and have a bigger-picture focus. Because this is the 'big picture' for you, you have elevated it to the top of the list by placing three dots in front of the word "Project." This higher priority increases the likelihood you will complete this task because it creates a reminder for you to keep those big-picture goals moving forward.

..ACTIONS. This is a list for tasks you need to complete, independent of other actions, so list the very next physical step for an item you must move forward.

..CALLS. This is a subcategory of ..ACTIONS. When entering a call to be made, enter the person's name, subject matter and phone number. This category is optional and is reserved for those people with whom you do not speak frequently and regularly.

..TEAM. This is the place to capture items you need to discuss with members of your team. For this list to work effectively, begin each new task item with the name or initials (be sure to use the same thing each time) of the person you need to work with so that the tasks will sort together when you alphabetize the list. This will make it easier to review tasks when you are talking with each of your team members.

(*For managers*: This is a good place to list the specific items and topics you need to discuss with team members during one-on-one meetings.)

..WAITING FOR. This category contains information promised to you by someone else. Until they perform their work and get back to you, you cannot do anything else on that item. Track items you have delegated to other people or items you are waiting to hear back on from clients or team members here. This category allows you to keep a clear head about what you can act on and what you cannot because you are waiting for someone else. For example, after completing the presentation, I forwarded it to my vendor for their additions. It will not be complete to send to the client until the vendor finishes their piece.

.. **(MANAGER'S NAME)** . In the blank space, enter your manager's name. Here you capture items to discuss with your manager, either in person or on the phone. (*Note*: It's a great tool to use for performance reviews. It allows you to go back and review those items you have completed as well as your timeliness. It's also a great tool for you to demonstrate your effectiveness with your manager!)

If you are self-employed, you might use this category to track your communication with your key contact for major clients. For example, if ABC Company is your biggest client and Mary is your main point of contact, you might use a ...Mary category to track the things you need to discuss with her.

.ERRANDS. This list contains the *ACTIONS* you must perform away from the office and home, i.e., pick up office supplies, get oil changed or pick up dry cleaning. Having all of your errands in one place ensures you are maximizing your time while you are out and about. If you have to wait while one errand is being completed, there may be another errand you can accomplish close by – like picking up the dry cleaning from around the corner while you wait for the oil to be changed in your car.

.HOME. This lists those *ACTIONS* you need to do while at home, especially those you're reminded of when you're at your office. This list helps you stay focused while at work and provides you with one place to look for the things you need to take care of when you are at home.

.READ/REVIEW. Reading and reviewing written materials for your work can easily overwhelm you, simply by the sheer volume. This category allows you to log important reading so it is distinguished from other reading, such as interest and leisure. This is an optional category. Use it if you have quite a few items to read or review that aren't important enough to merit listing on the ..ACTIONS list. I use it to keep track of the business articles I don't want to miss.

.SOMEDAY/MAYBE. This category is for the ideas, future projects or "maybe someday I'll get to that, but not now" list. These are things you are interested in doing, but don't have the time, money, energy or resources. The job of this list keeps the creativity flowing as your ideas incubate.

TRY IT – Categorize your Tasks

1. In your PIM software, determine how you can create categories or keywords to group the items on your task list. If your PIM software doesn't have a categories feature, you can use keywords by preceding each new task with the appropriate keyword and a colon. For example, you would begin each task that is something you need to do with ..ACTION.

2. Look at the task list you created earlier in the Mind Sweep exercise and apply the appropriate category or code to each task. You may need to customize the view of the task list so

that you can see the category or code name and then sort by it. You may also need to re-write the items or ensure that you have listed the actual very next *ACTION* on your list.

Take your time as you are setting up the system to make sure that you build strong habits. You will get faster quickly.

You've:

♦ cleared your head,

♦ narrowed where you are collecting data,

♦ learned a decision-making model to process each item, and

♦ organized your work in your PIM software.

You're well on your way to being a Thriving Professional. Now, for the next step – **Executing**.

CHAPTER 6

GETTING THE RIGHT THINGS DONE:

EXECUTING

There is time enough for everything, in the course of the day,
if you do but one thing at once; but there is not time enough in the year,
if you will do two things at a time.

– Philip Dormer Stanhope, 4th Earl Chesterfield

As you envision implementing The Effective EDGE – and the difference it will make in your life – think about the following questions: How do you control the pace of your day? How do you prioritize? How can you create an environment so that you can focus on your work? How do you keep your energy – mental and physical – high all day?

There are a variety of strategies you can integrate into your routine to ensure you are being as productive as possible. Each one takes minimal effort but can reap maximum rewards.

BATCHING YOUR E-MAIL

Most all of our organizations use "batching" for simple tasks like taking all the checks received in the mail that day to the bank at one time or backing up the servers at 2 a.m. – rather than all day. Batching saves you precious time whenever you find yourself doing repetitive operations – like processing your e-mail.

Most of us open up our PIM software in e-mail – and stay there except for the occasional moments when we are checking our calendars or looking up a phone number. Studies tell us that the more time we spend in e-mail, the less productive we are.

Processing your e-mail in batches rather than sitting in your e-mail inbox all day helps you make decisions faster about each new item. Batching your e-mail lets you focus on a decision of either **delete** (or file), **do it, delegate** or **defer** within 8-10 seconds for one e-mail.

Once you have processed your e-mail using the batching method, then you can begin to manage your day from your calendar and *ACTIONS* list instead of just reacting to new e-mails all day. Batching allows you to stay focused

Remember in the Introduction how we talked about writing with the other hand? This may feel like writing with the "wrong" hand. It's also one habit that will likely change the way you work **and** your experience of work – and for the better!

Larry and Marcus were used to reacting. E-mail was just one of the numerous ways in which they reacted. Each found it difficult to change because every time they returned from a meeting they wanted to "check" their e-mail. Each time they did, no decision was made about the new items they received. At best, they thought about something else that increased their anxiety. Shifting to batching actually made them each feel better about how they approached their work.

WARM-UP FOR YOUR DAY

Athletes would never imagine just running onto the court and beginning a game. They warm up their muscles and review their game plan. In many ways, we are like these athletes. We can learn a few things from them as we Execute our work.

In my years of working with some of this country's top executives, I've found one of the greatest challenges we all face is starting each workday in a productive way. Surprised? As soon as we arrive at the office, we're bombarded. E-mails, meetings, interruptions. Marcus referred to it as the "human pinball syndrome" – bouncing from crisis to crisis, from the minute he walked in the door until the time he left. He never felt in control and simply reacted to whatever happened next, often missing meetings or conference calls because he started his day reacting to his e-mail, realizing he should have been in a meeting 10 minutes ago.

To avoid the "human pinball" syndrome or missing those meetings, start your day with a Warm-Up! Beginning your day with clarity and a little preparation ensures that as you go through your day, you are aware of the big picture, of what you have already committed to and are best able to respond to the e-mails and events that might have happened overnight.

The Effective EDGE "Warm-Up" is straightforward and, typically, takes only a few minutes. Many of my clients schedule a recurring appointment for themselves the first 30 minutes of each day so that others don't schedule meetings during their Warm-Up time. During this time, they perform the following steps to prepare for the day ahead:

1. Unpack anything you took home or on the road. Put loose paper in your In tray. Boot your computer. Get water.

(Staying hydrated is key to maintaining your energy throughout the day.)

2. Review your calendar and task list to ensure that the time-specific and date-specific agreements you have made can be kept. Many PIM software programs have a view where you see all of your appointments and tasks for the day in one place. *Note:* This is a much better place than your e-mail inbox to begin evaluating what's ahead of you today.

3. Download your voice mail since, typically, the most urgent items from overnight will be there.

4. Process your e-mail inbox. Remember: Don't just check your messages; use the 4D's (Delete It, Do It, Delegate It, Defer It) to clear it out!

5. Process your paper In tray.

6. Ensure you have the materials you need for any meetings. If needed, print agendas, paperwork, directions or other items you need so you aren't scrambling to prepare a few minutes before the meeting.

7. Review your ..ACTIONS list for any key tasks due in the next few days. If time allows, begin tackling those tasks today.

8. Begin the day!!!

Marcus and I worked to integrate this Warm-Up routine into the start of his day. He scheduled a 30-minute appointment on his calendar, beginning at 8 a.m. Both he and his assistant made a pledge to cancel that meeting only in a true emergency.

Marcus now starts each day by reviewing appointments and tasks he's already promised to deliver on that day and what he needs to do to meet his goals. Before he makes new commitments, he becomes clear on the commitments he has already made. He has shifted his perspective from being reactive to being proactive and focused.

TRY IT: Warm-up for Your Day Calendar Appointment

Schedule a recurring, 30-minute meeting for yourself at the start of each weekday so you have time to take steps to begin your day deliberately.

1. Explore your PIM software to find out how to view your calendar and task list, side-by-side, for a particular day. Many PIM programs have a "Home" or "Today" view so you focus on your appointments and tasks that are due.

2. At the start of each day, use The Effective EDGE to begin your day deliberately.

HITTING YOUR STRIDE: EXECUTING: THE CRITICAL PIECE

Once you've started your day, move forward on your goals throughout the day, even as you receive new tasks and demands. To meet your objectives for the day, keep your head clear and manage your activities for the day from your calendar and task list, not from your head.

Remember Susan, the surgeon, wife and mother? She was juggling a number of demanding roles and wanted to be successful in all of them. Each one required numerous tasks, and she was trying to manage all of this in her head. When Susan began using The Effective EDGE, she was able to clear her head so she could focus on the larger issues in front of her. And by using it throughout the day, she was able to envision and manage her next *ACTIONS*.

For some, checking your list once or twice each day is sufficient. Others may want to check their lists more often. There is no need to "over check," but do check often enough to feel on track. As you receive new information, apply the 4D's and put deferred items on your calendar or task list.

As you complete items, mark them off the task list. Remember: Until you acknowledge an item has been accomplished, you can't reclaim your full energy from that task. Take the time to recognize the task is done before you move on to the next *ACTION* on your list.

CREATE THIS MINDSET AND YOU WILL GET THINGS DONE!
As you work with The Effective EDGE, how do you determine what to do next? The next obvious step is "prioritization." It is simpler than you think – more intuitive and doesn't take time from your day!

Many of us prioritize by sitting down with our list of *ACTIONS* and assigning a letter or number system to represent what we'll do first, second, third, etc. Larry spent 15 minutes every day prioritizing his list.

The problem with Larry's prioritization, however, was that it didn't make room for the new and unexpected events that happened during his day – and they always happened. The first time the phone rang or an e-mail arrived, Larry's previous priorities would change and the 15 minutes he'd spent making the list was wasted. He would start at the beginning of the day and give up his prioritization as the day went on. Larry's prioritization system was no longer practical, flexible enough or moved fast enough for the pace of his job.

With The Effective EDGE, Larry started prioritizing as soon as he started organizing. He cleared any reference information out of the way by asking the question, "Is it actionable?" for each new piece of information he received. This question allowed him to remove approximately half of the items and information he received by dumping it or filing it immediately. Only the items that required action were left to evaluate.

Then, he took action on any item that required two minutes or less to perform. This cleared another 30 percent of the information he received out of the way so he could focus on more involved tasks.

Next, Larry took the 20 percent that is left and either delegated it to someone else if able or deferred the rest to his *ACTIONS* in his calendar and task list. A key to effectively prioritizing is having all your promises, reminders and commitments listed in front of you with real due dates.

When using The Effective EDGE, your highest priority items are those that can only be performed on or are due today. You have reminded yourself of these items during your Warm-Up to prepare for your day. You will perform those tasks first.

Once you've completed the must-dos for the day, evaluate your *ACTIONS* list to decide on what to accomplish next. There, in one place, you have all the tasks and information that is critical to decide, including due dates. Rather than spending non-productive time assigning numbered or lettered codes to your tasks, use the

TEST criteria to determine which *ACTION* you are going to do next. The *TEST* will help leverage your available time whenever you have an open window of time, no matter how small.

Time – How much time do you have? If you only have 10 minutes, don't try to start a two-hour task.

Energy – How much energy do you have? Look for a task on your list that matches your current energy level. Your mental and physical energy move up and down numerous times during the day. If your energy is low, then it's probably not a good idea to contact a customer, but rather to call a peer about the report format or schedule your annual physical.

Setting – Where are you? What tools do you have available? If you are waiting in an airport with no Wi-Fi connection, you can't download and answer e-mails or log in and complete the HR reports. What can you tackle on your list in that location and context?

Top Level – What is the highest leverage action you can take at this moment? If you have the time, energy and are in the right situation to perform three tasks, which task is the highest leverage? Which task moves the most people toward their goal if you do it right now?

Since you are managing from your lists instead of your head, tasks don't fall off the radar screen or get lost. They also aren't forgotten because you left them in your head. They get done when the time is right. Have 10 minutes before a meeting starts? Great! Look at your list and determine what you can do in 10 minutes. Your focus is on how you can be productive in this moment.

TRY IT: Put your *ACTIONS* to the *TEST*

1. View your *ACTIONS* list.

2. If you had 30 minutes to work on any item, what would be your first priority? Take the *TEST*!

3. What if you don't have access to the Internet or your network?

At first, even though Larry's numbering prioritization wasn't working, he was uncomfortable giving it up. He quickly found that The Effective EDGE allowed him to spend more time being productive and, not surprisingly, he was getting more done. He also found taking the *TEST* gave him greater flexibility to complete the things on his list at a time that was appropriate.

Ultimately, Larry became a master of finding something he could accomplish – no matter the amount of time. He was utilizing each window of time, and his productivity soared.

The time you invest in maintaining steady, forward motion will be repaid through greater accomplishment and success.

♦ Start your day deliberately with the Warm-Up.

♦ Manage from your list and not your head.

♦ Acknowledge your completions.

♦ Focus instead of multitasking.

♦ Prioritize using the *TEST*.

These five practices can have an enormous impact on your productivity. You are focused, and your attention is on accomplishment and completion, not on maintaining a priority list that changes every time the phone rings or a new e-mail arrives.

Your focus is on what you have to deliver rather than responding to your e-mail. You are in control of your day instead of it controlling you.

Empty, Decide, Group and Execute to thrive!

CHAPTER 7

5 Steps in 5 Minutes:

Project Planning Made Easy

You've got to think about big things while you're doing small things, so that all the small things go in the right direction.

– Alvin Toffler

For most of us, we don't need the level of planning and detail used for the space shuttle project. In fact, most of our projects are smaller pieces of a bigger initiative. Or they fall into the realm of hiring a sales manager, rolling out a new product, completing performance reviews, finalizing budgets or putting in a new back yard. Yet, many times, we choose a level of planning that doesn't fit the task.

At the same time, many of us feel challenged to stay motivated to achieve our goals while completing our day-to-day tasks. Why? Because we get bogged down in the details of our work and forget about the big picture, which is our main motivation in the first place.

The late management guru Peter Drucker said, "To make knowledge productive, we will have to learn to see both the forest and trees. We will have to learn to connect them."

This was the challenge Larry faced. He was putting in long hours and doing lots of work, but he had lost sight of the big picture. He was performing the individual tasks, but because he wasn't focused on his desired outcome, the tasks weren't getting him the results he needed. He was taking steps, but wasn't reaching his desired destination. Therefore, he was unable to see the forest ... or the trees, for that matter. He just felt like he was living in the weeds.

Marcus also found himself too focused on the day-to-day and managing from crisis to crisis. Often he had forgotten what he was expected to deliver. He had no system to help him direct his energy. Instead, he did whatever popped in front of him next, whether it was moving him forward or not.

Imagine that the forest is the big picture of our work and lives, the 30,000-ft. aerial view of what we are trying to accomplish. The trees are the projects that are significant parts of our forest. To thrive, we need a way to stay connected to the big picture as a whole and also stay focused on the trees in our entire forest. Many times we stay focused on one or two trees and forget the rest. We need to focus – and nurture – all of them. Yet, many times we are down in the weeds – so to speak.

To see all of our big-picture items, we create Projects using the "...PROJECTS" category. Projects are often our strategic work – the deliverables resulting from our annual goals, our development plans and our client assignments.

Project tasks are more detailed than individual tasks, representing larger assignments with more than five steps. Many Projects are traditional projects with a start and end date. But you also may have projects that are ongoing in nature or that are goal-oriented, meaning that the Project is complete when the goal is achieved, not after a certain time has expired. For example, you may have a new habit that you are integrating or a company initiative that you want to stay focused on, but for which you do not have a specific timeframe.

Creating a Project task is similar to the down-and-dirty plan you might do on the back of an envelope. It's a quick, five-step sequence you can do in five minutes. The purpose? To provide yourself a place to design and detail your goal, empty your head of all the details and tie them to the day-to-day tasks in front of you.

In this chapter, you will create a task for each Project. Again, these can be professional or personal Projects for items as varied as completing the budget for your group, repainting the house or preparing for the annual offsite.

Some who use PIM software think they've lost a place to design projects. Using the Project task sequence will help regain the focus you need for your strategic work.

We are not suggesting that you replace other project management tools, but we are asking that you at least spend five minutes creating a Project task in your PIM software so that you can refer to this big-picture item. This will help you make effective decisions about the new things you can take on.

STEP 1: CREATE A PROJECT TASK

Let's make it simple:

- ◆ Review your list of tasks for items that can be categorized as a Project.

- ◆ Do they have more than 5 steps?

- ◆ Are they big-picture items that will help you meet your goals for the year?

- ◆ Change the category on each of these tasks to …PROJECT to move it up in your task list.

STEP 2: WRITE A DESIRED OUTCOME

Next, write a desired outcome. The desired outcome is a powerful tool because it helps you focus on where you are going, making you more effective.

The desired outcome is a clear, inspirational statement of what the project will look and feel like when completed. It is written, not just with our heads – which create linear, objective statements – but also with our hearts and gut so it includes emotion and intuition.

Author Robert K. Cooper says, in his book *The Other 90%*, "It is our heart, not our head, that plays the dominant role in moving us to excel. If we do not feel our outcomes, we cannot live them."

The desired outcome helps build that motivation into each project.

The desired outcome is written in the present and as a positive statement, as if it is already happening.

Here's a sample of a traditional outcome statement and a desired outcome:

Traditional Outcome Statement
Develop a 5-minute digital presentation and overview of The Effective Edge's new online courses — the 2-hour refresher course and the stand-alone, 4-hour interactive version of Getting the Edge.

Desired Outcome Statement
Develop a lively and engaging 5-minute digital presentation of The Effective Edge's new online courses – the 2-hour refresher course and stand-alone, 4-hour interactive version of Getting the Edge that encourages both current and prospective clients to utilize the programs within their organizations. The presentation represents The Effective Edge's reputation as the cutting-edge organization for productivity improvement.

Which one would you want to be a part of?

Athletes use this type of visualization to be successful. They picture themselves doing whatever is necessary to win the race or the game before they ever step onto the track or the court. They see themselves making each catch, scoring each point and taking each step to the successful outcome. They see themselves successfully crossing the finish line. They can see it in their minds and feel it in their bodies!

We can easily apply the same concept to our work. One client, a leading consumer goods corporation, used this idea of the desired outcome very successfully in one of their departments.

The Vice President challenged his team to create the cover for the *Wall Street Journal* on the day they reached their goal in five years. Each team member hung a copy of the mock-up newspaper in their office to remind them of what they wanted from the project, using it to inspire and motivate during challenging days.

By setting our Desired Outcome, we keep our eye on the big picture while we perform each of the small steps to get there. We also ensure we are fully engaged in our work.

STEP 3: PERFORM A PROJECT MIND SWEEP

Once the Desired Outcome is written, brainstorm a list of tasks you will need to complete for the Project. The list doesn't have to be in any particular order and doesn't even have to use the *ACTIONS* criteria we discussed earlier. The idea is to give you a place to clear your head of all the details of the project.

This step gives you an opportunity to brainstorm the steps if you don't have another tool to organize the work. Continue to add items to this list as they pop into your head during the course of the project. If you have the details of the project stored in another tool – like a GANTT chart or a spreadsheet – you don't need to re-create those steps in your PIM software.

STEP 4: LIST PROJECT DOCUMENTS

Now, list the documents you will need during the course of the project. Having a list in your Project task makes it easy to locate and refer to the documents. You want to be able to easily refer to the organizing documents of the Project, like a detailed spreadsheet timeline or the document for evaluations you need to complete.

Some PIM applications allow you to create links to these documents – called hyperlinks – which makes it easy to open them from within the Project task.

Note: This is different than attaching copies of the documents to the Project task. Attachments create a separate copy of the document, which require much greater storage space and are not updated when the main file is changed.

STEP 5: WRITE THE NEXT *ACTION* IN A NEW TASK ITEM

After you have created the Project's desired outcome, performed a Project Mind Sweep and created a document list, close the task in which you are working. Create a new task for the *very* next *ACTION* to be taken.

As you work through your Projects, these "next *ACTIONS*" serve as a "bookmark" of where you are in the Project.

Think of it this way: If you are reading a book and are interrupted, you don't just put the book down or you'd lose your place. Instead, you use a bookmark so when you come back, you can easily find your place.

The next *ACTION* serves as a bookmark for your Project – exactly where you need to pick up when you return.

When you have completed the next *ACTION* for the Project, mark it "complete" in your task list and in the Mind Sweep list of your Project task. Many PIM software applications allow you to apply the strikethrough so you can mark it out. Or, you could place a large "X" next to the task in the Mind Sweep list of your Project to indicate that it's complete.

Next, identify the next *ACTION* for that Project and add it to your task list, adding a category and a due date, if there is one.

TRY IT: 5 Steps in 5 Minutes: Create a Project Task

1. Create a Project Task. Identify a Project in your current task list or create a new Project task. Don't forget to categorize it as a "…PROJECT."

2. Write a Desired Outcome statement for the Project. Remember to state it in the present tense and use a little heart and gut when you write it.

3. Perform a Project Mind Sweep to create a list of the steps to complete the Project.

4. Make a list of the project documents – use hyperlinks if your PIM software allows.

5. Determine what the very next *ACTION* is for the Project and create a task for that *ACTION*.

Review each Project at least once each week to refocus your attention on your desired outcome and where you are in achieving your goal. This Project design will motivate you through your desired outcome and allow you to manage your day-to-day tasks through the *ACTIONS* on your task list.

For Larry and Marcus, adding the Project focus shifted their perspectives toward their goals and ensured that each of the *ACTIONS* they took moved them toward the completion of that goal or project. They not only became more focused, but felt more accomplished and energized, as well.

Using this practice will help you not only achieve, but regularly surpass your goals as a Thriving Professional.

CHAPTER 8

THE WEEKLY RECHARGE:

MAINTAINING YOUR EDGE

Quality is never an accident; it is always the result of high intention,
sincere effort, intelligent direction and skillful execution;
it represents the wise choice of many alternatives.

– William A. Foster

Susan was overwhelmed by the details of her life. She found it difficult to focus on her objectives and to stay on top of the myriad of tasks that went along with each of her many roles. Was she overlooking an important deadline for the center's administration? Did she have everything she needed for her upcoming surgeries? Where were the kid's Halloween costumes?

Using The Effective EDGE adds something most programs and processes don't provide – The Weekly Recharge. By adding to her routine a time to reflect on what she'd accomplished and what was ahead, Susan built in time to look at her goals and the detailed actions needed to achieve them.

Think about the central air-conditioning in your home. Periodically, the Freon requires a recharge. The same goes for a battery that's been allowed to run down.

The Weekly Recharge provides maintenance for The Effective EDGE as well as a way to provide closure to the past week as you look forward to the next. It also provides the opportunity to catch something you might have missed so that it doesn't fall through the cracks.

To begin the Weekly Recharge, find one hour you can commit to each week. Most of the time, this review will require less than an hour, but blocking an hour gives you plenty of time to complete this all-important step without interruption.

Schedule the Weekly Recharge as a recurring appointment on your calendar and give yourself time to focus and think. Here are a few suggestions to support you in your Weekly Recharge.

- Close your door.

- Put your phone on "Do Not Disturb."

- Give yourself time to think.

STEP 1: LOOSE PAPER

- Take all of the scraps of paper, business cards, receipts, etc. tucked into your portfolios, note-taking device, briefcases, wallet or scattered on your desk and put them to your In tray.

- Process each piece of paper using the 4D's.

STEP 2: PROCESS YOUR NOTES & VOICE MAIL

- Review the notes in your note-taking device, meeting notes and notes scribbled from conversations, then process them using the 4D's – store phone numbers and contact information.

♦ Add items to your calendar or task list.

♦ Do the same with all of your voice mail.

♦ Make sure each item has been handled appropriately and your voice mailbox is empty.

STEP 3: E-MAIL

♦ Process all of the e-mail in your inbox, using the 4D's.

♦ Leave your inbox totally clear. Taking time to clear your inbox reassures you that each item has been handled, items needed for reference are stored in the right place and you can quickly locate and identify action items.

STEP 4: CALENDAR
Prior Week:

♦ Review, in detail, the recent week's calendar.

♦ Acknowledge the items you have completed.

♦ Renegotiate any open *ACTION* items that you have not yet completed and reschedule any appointments.

♦ Take time to appreciate all that you were able to achieve during the last week.

Upcoming Events:

♦ Review your upcoming calendar events, both long- and short-term.

♦ Create any action items needed to prepare for upcoming events.

♦ Review your next week to ensure that you know what you need to do to be completely successful.

♦ Renegotiate any events or *ACTION* items if necessary.

STEP 5: REVIEW PROJECT & OUTCOME LISTS

♦ Review the Projects on your task list.

♦ Evaluate desired outcomes and the status of each project.

♦ Ensure at least one current *ACTION* item is listed on your task list for each Project.

♦ Remember, the more you review your outcomes, the greater the likelihood you will achieve them!

STEP 6: MIND SWEEP

♦ Add any actions or projects that you have been keeping in your head to your task list or calendar.

♦ Store those actions in your PIM software where they belong.

STEP 7: CHECK FOR UNCATEGORIZED TASKS & UNSENT E-MAILS

♦ Check your e-mail folders to ensure you haven't saved an e-mail that you meant to send. Unsent e-mails are often stored in a Drafts or Work in Progress folder by your PIM software.

♦ Review your task list.

♦ Each action stored should be assigned a category.

STEP 8: REVIEW *ACTION* LISTS

♦ Mark off completed items from each of the *ACTION* lists.

♦ Move finished tasks to the completed items folder or delete them so they don't clutter up the list.

♦ Review your future actions.

♦ Set reminders to help you accomplish those tasks on time.

♦ Celebrate your accomplishments!!

Once you've marked an item as "complete," you may want to delete it or move it into a Completed Tasks folder rather than leave it on the main task list. Not only does this clean up the clutter on your list, but it also helps when it's time to conduct performance reviews or you need a year-end summary of accomplishments.

STEP 9: REVIEW PAPER FILES & SUPPORT FILES

♦ Browse through all paper support materials for your work in progress.

♦ Create tasks or appointments for any new actions you might think of during this review.

♦ Throw away or file in long-term reference any materials that you no longer need in your working files.

STEP 10: REVIEW YOUR "SOMEDAY/MAYBE" LIST

♦ Scan through your Someday/Maybe list to see if there is anything that you are now willing to commit the time, energy and resources to achieving.

♦ Has one of your Someday/Maybes become a new Project?

STEP 11: BE CREATIVE & COURAGEOUS

♦ Add to your system any new, creative, thought-provoking, risk-taking ideas to which you are ready to commit.

♦ Take some time to explore your ideas and think beyond your day-to-day tasks.

TRY IT: Schedule Your Weekly Recharge

1. Review your calendar and schedule a recurring, weekly, one-hour appointment for your Weekly Recharge. Many people find that Friday afternoon before 3 p.m. is a good time for their review so they have time to finish any uncompleted items.

2. At the time of the review, take out the list above and perform each step.

The Weekly Recharge is the most important meeting you have each week. Effectively having this meeting ensures every other meeting, *ACTION*, call and conversation I have the following week supports moving my big picture forward. I am more flexible and not thrown off course and out of balance when "pebbles" or "boulders" are tossed into my pond. My mind stays more like calm water.

The Weekly Recharge is an incredible tool to help keep your system going. Recharging yourself and The Effective EDGE will give you peace of mind knowing what you've accomplished and what is on the horizon.

INCUBATION VS. PROCRASTINATION

Many of us try to complete everything we think of, regardless of whether we can actually do it. As you perform the Weekly Recharge, you may notice that you've been skipping items on your task list.

Most of us pass over items for one of two reasons. Either it is not the right time to complete the item or we are procrastinating. To figure out which one it is, ask these questions:

Are you committed to the task?

In order to accomplish anything, you must have the time, money, energy and resources. If you don't, you will spin your wheels. If the answer is "no," then renegotiate to remove the task from your list or move it to your Someday/Maybe list. If you aren't committed to it, don't add it to your list. You lose energy and focus when you have things on your list that you aren't clearly committed to seeing through.

By using the Someday/Maybe list, you keep your head clear and let the item incubate until it is time and you have all the resources necessary. You are also freeing energy to fully focus on those items for which you do have the time, money, energy and resources to accomplish now.

Are you procrastinating?

If you are unable to commit to the task, then determine why you are putting it off. We are either apathetic about the task or we have anxiety about it. Apathy often occurs when we have tedious, time-consuming or repetitive tasks to perform – expense reports commonly fall into this category. It is difficult to be enthusiastic about expense reports, and people often put them off until the last minute or until they're overdue.

Focusing on the desired outcome is a good way to stay motivated, even when dealing with the most mundane tasks. Review the desired outcome to remind yourself of how this action fits into the big picture you're trying to accomplish. If you still need a boost to get started, break the task into small, manageable bites. Often, once you get started on something, it's easier to keep the momentum going.

The other common cause of procrastination is anxiety. This can be caused by having a large, complex assignment, having to do something that is distasteful or emotional or fear of failure.

Once again, by breaking the assignment into manageable pieces, you can begin gaining momentum and moving forward. When dealing with an unpleasant task, focus on the desired outcome, a sort of spoonful of sugar needed to make the distasteful medicine go down.

Before I have difficult employee development conversations, I remind myself of the positive outcome that I'm trying to achieve for that employee's progress – and for the company. Bottom line, it gives a positive purpose to a strenuous conversation.

Regardless of the cause of the procrastination, as you identify tasks you've been avoiding, take time to make them more manageable, breaking them into smaller pieces and then linking them back to the desired outcome.

The Weekly Recharge is one of your best tools to establish and sustain that feeling of relaxed control. If you perform your Weekly Recharge on Friday, you head into the weekend knowing that you have a good handle on things and that you are prepared for the week ahead – giving you the freedom to thrive in your personal life.

For Susan, the Weekly Recharge gave her the much-needed confidence that she was doing the right things at the right time. She was now able to enjoy her time with her family instead of worrying about what she might have missed at the hospital.

Reflect, recharge and thrive!

CHAPTER 9

YOUR WORD – YOUR ENERGY:

KEEPING AGREEMENTS

The man who promises everything is sure to fulfill nothing.

– Carl Gustav Jung

Ever drive through heavy fog and wonder if you will reach your destination? It can take extra energy and even be exhausting. Being unclear of when things are due is much like driving in the fog. Having a clear picture of everything that you have promised to deliver is like having the fog lift. It clears the roadway, breaks up the clouds and provides a clear path in which to drive clearly toward your goals and outcomes, promises and commitments.

One way to maintain 100 percent visibility of your goals and the tasks needed to achieve them is first to have them all listed in one place where they are easily accessible. You need to avoid making promises that you can't keep. If you make too many agreements, you may not only drop the ball on your current task, but you may end up dropping the ball on other tasks, as well.

Eager to prove herself, Beth agreed to all of the projects that came
her way. She took on more than she could ever accomplish, trying
to let her boss and co-workers know she was a valuable and
enthusiastic team member.

Marcus, on the other hand, was taking on too much because he
was hesitant to delegate to his team. He had delegated in the past
and others hadn't delivered. He couldn't afford to get burned
anymore. Instead, he tried to carry the whole load himself.

How many of us hesitate to delegate to others because they have
broken a previous commitment?

Have you ever broken a promise to yourself?

You may have planned to get up and work out in the morning,
finish your expense reports tomorrow, get that big project done by
the end of the month or start eating a healthier diet next week.
Then, life happens and for whatever reason, and you don't get
around to doing what you said. We can feel bad – or guilty – for
not following through. This can shake our confidence and self-
esteem, which is a critical foundation for us as professionals. To
know what promises we have made, to be able to see how all of those
merge together and to be able to orchestrate the completion of
them is critical to our success. When we deliver, we feel successful
and accomplished, wanting to take on more. When we don't, we
frequently want to contract and take on a safer or smaller promise.

How often have you avoided a colleague or customer because you
haven't met a deadline or completed a task you agreed to do?

If you agree to take on something new, be willing to make that
commitment with 100 percent of yourself. When you aren't truly

committed, you have a greater propensity to break your promises – and this affects your ability to work with others. In turn, this may impact your self-esteem, your willingness to take on new things, and it may reduce your level of trust in yourself and others. The stakes are subtle and high!

Want to reduce your internal conflict from broken promises? Here's how:

Record all of your agreements. Sometimes you don't even realize you've broken a promise. For example, when someone calls and you say, "I will call you right back," you return to what you were doing and forget to call back because you didn't write it down. When you make a promise to yourself, a colleague, friend or family, write it down!

A Chinese proverb says, "The palest ink is better than the brightest memory." Capture each commitment in your PIM software. Then, you'll be less likely to break a promise that is recorded.

Marcus could have felt more comfortable delegating if his staff had been recording the promises they made and he had kept track of those commitments himself.

We need to record not only the promises we make but also the agreements others make with us. If we are tracking what someone promised us, then we're more likely to follow up in a timely manner. Use the "..WAITING FOR" category to keep track of promises others have made to you.

Make fewer agreements. It is okay to say "no" when you are overloaded. You will now have a good system in which you can better evaluate your current workload before committing to something else. If we decline a task, we may worry that our manager or colleagues will be upset with us. The reality is, if you can't get the work done without sacrificing the quality of the product or your health and welfare, then it's better to decline the assignment. It's best not to come up short when the deadline is hours or minutes away. Saying "no" when the task is due causes much more damage and has greater consequences and negative results than telling someone you are overcommitted when first asked.

With The Effective EDGE, you have all of your current agreements in front of you so you will know your capacity for any new commitments.

Beth had no system for keeping track of the projects she had already signed on to, so when approached about taking on something new, she couldn't accurately evaluate her ability to deliver. She was also afraid to say "no," thinking it would impede her progress in the company and in her career. Since she wasn't sure what she had already promised because she hadn't written them all down in one place, she would say "yes" to almost everything.

With The Effective EDGE, she could better assess whether she could take on something new. She quit over-promising, under delivering and started keeping the commitments she made.

Be selective about the agreements you make. Sometimes we commit to things that take too much time and energy away from our other projects and tasks.

Because Beth took on so many projects, she often agreed to tasks that didn't move her or her team toward their goals. She would sit in executive team meetings and agree to lead an initiative, even though it didn't synchronize with the deliverables for her team.

Instead, because they had spent so much time on non-related tasks, she and her team would struggle to meet their objectives as deadlines loomed.

Keep your agreements. Master keeping commitments – the ones you make with others and the ones you make with yourself. Promises you make to yourself are as important as the ones you make with others – and promises to yourself are usually the first promises broken.

Marcus would walk through the plant and take on every new problem he saw, such as a piece of equipment needing to be repaired or a process problem to be addressed. Because he didn't have a system for tracking his current commitments, he just kept piling on new tasks and nothing was ever accomplished.

And he was also breaking promises at home. He would ask the boys if they wanted to ride bikes on Saturday, but then would forget to put it on his calendar. When Saturday came around, he was at the office instead of cycling through the park with his sons.

Re-negotiate agreements. If, for any reason, you can't keep your agreement, re-negotiate the agreement at the earliest possible opportunity. Re-negotiating is not breaking a promise. When you know you aren't going to meet a deadline, contact your customer or colleague at the first sign of delay. It is better to negotiate a new due date than to deliver a sub-standard product or to miss a deadline.

Note: Be careful that you don't re-negotiate too often. If you begin re-negotiating deadlines on every project, you become the professional "who cried wolf" and you lose credibility.

Susan made agreements with herself about when she would get all the household and family needs taken care of, but kept them on a separate calendar at the house and couldn't access them from her office. When she couldn't meet these self-imposed deadlines, she would mentally reprimand herself.

The unfinished tasks would gnaw at her, making her feel guilty. With The Effective EDGE, she learned it was okay to have tasks and projects with no deadlines. She also knew to use the Someday/Maybe list for things she wanted to remember to do but didn't have the time, money, energy or resources to take on now.

Marcus also used the Someday/Maybe list to regain his focus. Because he needed to focus on the absolute must-dos and move everything else off his plate, he successfully re-negotiated with his boss to move all the non-essential projects to the side. Then, he used the Someday/Maybe list to keep track of the items he wanted to incubate and come back to when time was available.

As we begin keeping our agreements with ourselves and others, we feel a greater sense of accomplishment and success. We feel confident when we do what we say we will do, within the time frame we specified. And we have higher self-esteem because we know we aren't letting anyone down, including ourselves.

TRY IT: Using the EDGE to Keep Your Agreements

1. Review your task list and calendar. Add any promises or commitments you have made that are not reflected in your PIM software.

2. Review the deadlines for your commitments. Are they realistic? If not, re-negotiate now to ensure that you can deliver 100 percent on the commitments you have made. If there are items on your list that you are not committed to, then negotiate to remove them from your list.

3. Move any tasks that you want to do – but don't have the time, energy or resources to do now – to your Someday/Maybe list so they can incubate.

How can you get the EDGE on keeping your agreements?

CHAPTER 10

MANAGING INTERRUPTIONS:

THE X FACTOR

Circumstances may cause interruptions and delays,
but never lose sight of your goal.

– Mario Andretti

What's your "X" factor?

For many of us, the X-factor is not becoming more productive until the people around us allow us to be more productive. Instead, we find ourselves being constantly interrupted, impeding any chance of having time to focus on the projects in front of us.

Larry couldn't be proactive because he spent his days reacting to minor emergencies or answering questions from his staff who were sometimes lined up outside the door. He had no time during the week to look at the strategic and long-range tasks he needed to handle. Therefore, he worked late nights and weekends so he could dedicate any remaining energy to those tasks that would move the company to where he wanted it to be.

The anatomy of an interruption and the ensuing loss of productivity goes something like this:

- You are reviewing last week's sales and suddenly you think, "I need to talk to my colleague about the new changes to the weekly financial carry-forward report."

- This item is not an emergency, but something that popped into your head and interrupted your productivity – but you don't want to forget it.

- You would pick up the phone or go to your colleague's office and ask if they have a minute. Your colleague, wanting to be a good team member, says, "Sure!" This leads to a 5- to 10-minute conversation.

- While you are there, you might also discuss other work items or catch up on social news (how is the family, plans for the weekend.)

- In all, this conversation could take up to 10-15 minutes.

- When you get back to your desk, it takes you several more minutes to re-orient and to refocus on the action item you were working on before you interrupted yourself.

It takes the average professional 2-4 minutes to refocus after an interruption.

Calculate this: If you are interrupted a minimum of 15 times each day, you spend 30-60 minutes just refocusing. Spending one hour each day refocusing costs over $6,000 per year in lost productivity for a professional making $50,000. That's a lot of unproductive time and cost you can reclaim by better managing interruptions.

Larry desperately needed to recapture all of those minutes and focus better.

USING CATEGORIES TO MANAGE INTERRUPTIONS

The Effective EDGE helps you manage interruptions through the task categories.

The ..TEAM category helps you improve productivity and manage interruptions by providing an outlet for the source of most interruptions: your brain. Oftentimes, you will think of something you need to discuss with a team member while you are working on a totally unrelated task. If the item is not urgent, you can create a task to get the thought out of your head.

Put the team member's name or initials at the beginning of the task so you can easily identify who you want to discuss the item with, then categorize the task as a ..TEAM item. When you talk to that team member, you can then discuss anything else you have for them on your list. Using this method, you've decreased the number of interruptions for both of you and, at the same time, increased your productive time.

The second powerful category for managing interruptions is the ..WAITING FOR category. Many of us are hesitant to delegate, but with the ..WAITING FOR category, you can track what you have delegated so you can quickly refer back to it and follow-up.

When you delegate, create a task in your list for that item and categorize it as a ..WAITING FOR. Putting the person's name or initials at the beginning of the item can make it easier to identify what you need to review with them.

Remember: When you delegate, you want to delegate in writing, usually by e-mail, and include all of the necessary details, such as the due date, if there is one. The more specific your e-mail is that delegates the task, the more you can prevent interruptions asking for clarification.

The ..WAITING FOR category allows you to delegate with confidence because you can track the action. When you delegate, you give team members an opportunity to grow and be successful – experiences you want to encourage, not withhold.

By delegating, you also are allowing yourself to focus on the management aspect of your duties rather than the performance of the tasks.

TRY IT: Using the ..TEAM and ..WAITING FOR Categories

1. Review the items you have delegated to others and create tasks for them, using The Effective EDGE. Categorize each task with the ..WAITING FOR category. Start each item with the first name or initials of the person you delegated to so you can quickly locate items for them in your list.

2. Do a Mind Sweep exercise and clear your head of any items you want to discuss with your team. Document these items in your task list and group them under the ..TEAM category.

By effectively using the task categories, you can significantly increase your personal productivity. Like Larry, you can manage your interruptions and concentrate on the work that moves you, your team and your organization forward.

Focus and thrive!

CHAPTER 11

INTENTIONS:

THE ART OF CREATING WHAT YOU WANT

Our Intentions Create Our Reality

– Wayne Dyer

Most of us spend our lives reacting to what is in front of us rather than designing our lives so we can thrive. We spend months out of each year putting together goals and objectives, revenue figures and budgets for the company for which we work. But we spend very little time contemplating our life plan or creating intentions for our lives.

We may spend a few minutes, maybe even a few hours, deciding on our New Year's resolutions, but those quickly fade within the first few weeks. Creating Intentions supports us in thriving in all areas of our lives on an ongoing basis, not just today or this year.

Intentions are the overarching direction of our lives – like the rudder on a boat that keeps us on course. They connect us to our dreams, goals and desires even when the circumstances of life knock us off course. Clarifying our Intentions keeps us on track and keeps us from drifting out to sea.

WHATEVER YOU FOCUS ON, YOU GET MORE OF.
I quickly noticed a common thread through all of my clients' stories. They seemed to be working too hard to make things happen. They struggled too much, forcing things to happen. Most had given up on all but the day-to-day of their personal lives and worked extra hard to drive the business results needed.

They also had become very one-dimensional in their approach to work. They were working hard – and only working; not really living – or thriving!

I frequently ask my clients, "If you were productive, accomplished and effective in all areas of your life, how would you feel?"

When I posed this question to Susan, she immediately responded with "less stress!" That's the answer I get from most all my clients: Less of something.

Anyone who has children has probably said at one time or another, "***Don't*** spill the milk!" But, as you well know, they spill the milk.

My clients often say, "less stress." So, what do we get? Spilled milk and stress! Why? Because, whatever we focus on is what we get more of. So what are you focusing on? Lack of sleep, lack of money, not enough time, too much stress, problems, relationships that aren't working, the last team meeting that didn't go well?

So, what's really happening?

At the base of our skull is something called the Reticular Activating System (RAS). This is the messaging system that connects the brain and the rest of the body. When we engage both the brain and the body, we are, in essence, "fully engaged" in what we are creating. Our brains – in their basic form – are designed to have us be right. When we hear, "spill milk" or "stress," our brains, say, "Okay, I can do that."

Funny thing is, the brain doesn't understand when we want less of something or words like "don't." So, we have to tell our brains what we **do** want instead of what we **don't** want.

Using our RAS makes it easier to get what we want – and in a more organic and easy manner. When we harness this power, we can use it to create what we **do** want instead of feeling frustrated by getting more of what we **don't** want. This has been a powerful tool for each of my clients.

Marcus was worried sick he would be fired. He frequently found himself thinking about it, worrying about what would happen to his team, the region, his life and thinking about things that, literally, sent him into a downward spiral. He was almost paralyzed.

I asked what was his Intention?

"Well, not that!" came his immediate response. From there, we began to look at what he **did** want...and this helped him create this Intention: "With joy and ease, my team and I have turned this region around. We've gone from dead last to almost first within the year. Morale is high, retention is high and we are on track on revenues and safety. What a great time!"

As he stated the Intention he created, his demeanor changed. His energy soared and he had ideas he never imagined when he was focusing on getting fired.

Susan worried every day she wouldn't be able to hold things together. She could feel the stress in her body. We created this Intention for her: "My boundless energy is supporting me in living all my passions. My clients, family and I are receiving the benefits of my love and gentleness. All is taken care of with ease and minimal effort."

Once Susan and Marcus became aware that what they focused on was what they would get, they realized they had the power to fully engage with what they wanted – to create their own Intention. They had been letting their fears and worries create their realities. Now they had created powerful intentions, and that was becoming their reality.

MAKING OTHER'S INTENTIONS OUR OWN

Clients often find they are given goals to deliver on they didn't have a part in creating. In order to be fully engaged in making them happen, they need to make these goals their own. In their hearts, they may want to support these goals, but the goals just don't resonate because they aren't yet personal.

To thrive, you need all of your goals and Intentions to be your own, to be compelling, inspiring you to move them forward.

Creating an Intention engages our RAS. However, our RAS can only support us in what it understands. Some of us have gray, vague or conflicting Intentions. Take this Intention as an example: Grow sales by 30 percent over last year.

Our minds know what this means, but it requires us to decipher what is truly required to make it happen. Our bodies don't quite understand how to go about making it happen. The Intention isn't written in a way that's easily understood. By clarifying what we want to create, it makes it very easy for our entire body to respond – our brains and our bodies.

Before: Grow sales by 30 percent.

Now: With fun and enthusiasm, we are generating revenues of $4.7 million. Our clients are saying, "WOW. Our vendors are grateful for the additional work and we are having the time of our lives!"

Which Intention do you want to be a part of?

CREATING OUR INTENTIONS
The body cannot tell the difference between a well-imagined thought and reality.

Creating Intentions with The Effective EDGE aligns our mental, emotional, physical and spiritual dimensions. It connects head, heart and intuition, our left and right brains, our thoughts and our actions. It combines the objective and the subjective; the tangible and the experience we want to have.

From this creative and integrated place, our entire being works in harmony toward what we want and how we want our lives to unfold. There is more ease, grace, joy and love. When we are fully aligned, tasks are easier and can even happen faster than when we are out of balance, forcing things and only engaging parts of ourselves.

Creating Intentions with The Effective EDGE helps you take small, focused steps. It doesn't require any **more** effort, just focused and full-body effort.

One of the best aspects about an Intention is that you are telling your brain and body **what** you want. It will figure out the **how**. Once you have clearly identified your Intention, the RAS immediately begins to scan your environment for options, ideas and resources. This way, you don't have to worry and focus on the specifics of how this will happen. You focus and get clear on the **what** – the Outcome. The RAS focuses on the **how**.

1. **Identify the item for which you want to create an Intention.**
   Many of us aren't clear on what we want. In fact, we're clearer about what we don't want! Start by writing that down. Beth and I started our discussion with her saying she didn't want to just work all the time. She didn't want to be isolated from friends and family.

2. **Now identify what you DO want from the prior statement.**
   What is it your desire? Is it a promotion? A more cohesive team? Greater productivity? More money? A more balanced life? A lean, fit and strong body? Do you want to pursue and renew your photography hobby? As you consider what you want, write it in the present tense as if it is happening now. Write it as if you have that promotion, that lean and fit body or that new car. Be specific.

Beth massaged her words and came up with the following Intention:

> "I love my new position and being home in Texas. It's as if the job was created just for me. I've reconnected with most all my friends. I'm sleeping better, having lots more fun and keeping my job in balance. I feel a strong sense of health knowing I'm doing the right things for me on all levels."

3. Brainstorm or Mind-map the Intention You Desire.
Either inside the Outcome task or on a separate sheet of paper, create a "mind map" or "wishbone" of the different aspects of what you want. Create a Mind Sweep of all the ideas, resources and strategies that will support you in realizing your Intention. Once you have a complete list, begin to organize your results and identify other tasks that might be required. The idea is to get all of the ideas out of your head and onto paper so that you can see everything and make decisions about how you want to progress.

4. Energize Your Intentions. We all probably have months, years or decades of the habit of creating what we **don't** want. While it's a good start, we want to focus and energize what we **do** want to bring to life and our experience more quickly.

Here are a few ideas that you can use to ensure their Intentions become reality. They apply as well in the corporate world.

VISUALIZE YOUR INTENTION.
The saying, "One picture is worth a thousand words," is really true. One way to energize what you want is to create visual display. My favorite way is to take a 15 x 20 piece of black board and paste pictures and words from magazines that convey the Intention that I am creating.

Larry did this for his job and his life. He cut out a picture of a man, riding bikes with his kids, his desired salary, a picture of a calm pond (reflecting his calm demeanor at work) and a picture of a man and woman on a beach of a warm tropical island. He put it in his closet so that he could see himself in the image of his Outcome each and every morning. It took him about 15-20 seconds to imagine and energize his Intention and to really feel it!

Beth created a Visual Display about the job she wanted, the house where she could invite her friends and family over for an outdoor dinner and the activities she would be doing in her time away from work. She worked it until she saw herself in it.

AFFIRMATIONS – REPROGRAMMING THE MIND

Our minds seldom have original thoughts. We tend to latch onto a thought and then go down a long, dark rat hole of mischief, especially when something has happened we don't like. Most of those thoughts aren't supportive of what we truly want. Some of these thoughts are fear-based and even negative. Focusing on these can get us more of what we don't want. We need to interrupt those basic mental patterns with ones that we truly want for ourselves.

In order to interrupt that pattern – a habit some of us have lived for a long time – we can use affirmations.

An affirmation is a statement of what we want, stated in the present tense of the experience and Intention that we want to have. It is energizing and, at least, 50 percent believable.

Susan was always reprimanding herself for the things she wasn't doing well. Once she did this, her mind seemed to go on and on about all the other things she hadn't done well. Instead of objectively looking at how she could have done something better, the surgeon tended to make herself feel worse. The worse she felt, the more mistakes she made. It was a never-ending cycle.

Together, Susan and I created an affirmation she repeated several times each morning. She decided the affirmation was going to be gentle, supportive and uplifting. After just a week of saying the affirmation, she noticed when her mind was on automatic. She was repeating the affirmation over and over in her mind without consciously initiating it.

The best thing, though? Susan began, almost immediately, to experience herself being more successful at handling all the details.

Her affirmation: I am energized, in harmony with and successful at getting the right things done at the right time. I am at peace.

MENTAL REHEARSING

Use all your senses and imagine the event as if it's already happened. What does it feel like, smell like, look like? What are people saying to you, saying about you, what are you saying to yourself? Is it calm and peaceful around you, exhilarating and jubilant? Are you moving around, standing still? Where are you when this happens?

The best part of mentally rehearsing is that you can do it any time and any place. It takes just a second or two. Hold the image strongly until you can feel it throughout your entire body. Then let it go. Do this at least once a day and see the results!

5. **Take a Next *ACTION* and Course Correct.** Intentions are compelling. For me, I can barely keep myself from moving forward on them. I'm inspired and excited about what I am creating. I move forward, judiciously, by creating the next *ACTION* – as you learned in earlier chapters.

   After completing each *ACTION*, I step back and refine or "Course Correct." Despite clarifying our Intentions, creating Visual Displays, repeating Affirmations and Mentally Rehearsing, we can sometimes go off course. Unexpected obstacles arise and bump us off track.

If this happens, rather than abandon your Intention, take the time to re-examine it. As you "course correct," don't judge yourself for having to modify your initial plan. Few things in life manifest according to plan, and the flexibility to adapt your plans as your circumstances change – while still moving toward the Intention – is a key factor to thriving.

TRY IT: Create an Intention

Review your development plan, personal goals or the Projects you created earlier. Identify a major goal for which you would like to develop a deliberate plan.

1. **Identify your current state.**

2. **Write a clear Intention of what you choose to have.**

   Open a task in your PIM software and Categorize it in the …INTENTIONS category. Write a statement – in the present tense – focusing on what you want, rather than what you don't.

   ♦ Write 1-2 sentences. Allow yourself time to massage it into something that is worth your time, energy, money and resources. Make it come to life – with energy and enthusiasm!

   ♦ After you've written it, re-read it. Does it energize you? Do you feel engaged in the statement? Do you want to make this into a reality?

   ♦ If the answer is "yes," congratulations! If not, tweak it until it energizes you. Maybe you need to pick something bigger or smaller.

3. **Brainstorm or mind-map the Intention to energize it.**

4. **Energize your Intentions** by a Visual Display, Create an Affirmation and Mentally Rehearse seeing yourself successful in your Intention.

5. **Determine the next *ACTION*** and create a task or calendar item for it in your PIM software. As you complete each *ACTION*, Course Correct as necessary.

We are more likely to achieve our Intentions when we have clearly stated them and we are energized. Using The Effective EDGE, you are taking the time to be clear about your Intentions and are building an environment that supports you in reaching your goal.

Beth realized, using The Effective Edge, that she could be a greater asset to her company if she was true to her own Intentions. She began working with her managers to find a suitable position in the company's Texas offices so she could continue to contribute to the team while being true to her own needs.

Thriving Professionals use Intentions to create the reality that they want.

CHAPTER 12

BRINGING IT ALL TOGETHER

*To thrive: to grow vigorously : FLOURISH; to gain in wealth or possessions :
PROSPER; to progress toward or realize a goal despite
or because of circumstances.*

– Merriam-Webster Dictionary

Thriving looks different to each of us, but you know when you feel
like you are thriving. You have energy and buoyancy as you approach
each aspect of your day. You feel like the master, rather than the
slave, of your work and life.

For each of the professionals described in this book, thriving has
meant something different. And during their journey, they have all
stumbled or been out of balance for a brief period, then course
corrected to get back on track – even asking for help when they
needed it, so they could get back on track.

Larry's company acquired another mid-size technology company
and he has successfully integrated the management teams using
The Effective EDGE practices. Because he was clear and focused,
he was able to bring both companies together successfully.

He told me he couldn't have done it if his head hadn't been clear and the interruptions had continued. His ability to focus had allowed him to see the opportunity, capitalize on it and take a collaborative approach in how it all came together.

He's also established a better standard for his time and instituted polices to help his employees do the same. They now have "no-work weekends" and employees are encouraged to take Friday afternoons off between Thanksgiving and New Year's as well as during the summer.

It may seem to go against the grain of what many companies do, but Larry found – with these new policies – his employees work just as hard, are producing better results, morale has increased and employee loyalty has skyrocketed in the midst of a significant merger.

It has taken time, but Beth has realized that thriving is a complete package, not just being successful at work. She enjoys her job but recognizes an all-consuming job isn't enough – or right – for her. She now knows she has to be true to herself and look at the whole picture of where she wants to live and the kind of life she wants.

As of the printing of this book, she is in final interviews with a Texas-based company that plans to move her back to Texas, closer to friends and family.

Armed with her new tools to create an effective and powerful work life, Beth can now balance that with the rest of her life, ensuring it is just as potent. She is able to focus and understands the benefit and value of being clear on where she needs to invest her energy and where she doesn't. She's also able to use The Effective EDGE to maximize her productivity at work so she can begin building a life outside of work.

Marcus faced some real challenges, and it seemed that things got worse before they got better. Shortly after our work together he was put on a performance plan and given three months to turn things around. Instead of being fearful, he knew with his new skills he would turn the situation around.

Marcus is now thriving. After creating a strong leadership team, Marcus can take credit for someone reliable being available to field questions from plant personnel, 24/7. His reward: He no longer has to be on call around the clock ... and he now has the downtime he needs to be fresh and focused at work. He's also able to spend more time with his family, being the father and husband he really wants to be. His boss now counts on him as her strongest leadership team member. He is proud of the change he's created not only in his world, but that of his staff, plant, family and his boss.

Susan was juggling too many roles and had to find creative ways to outsource anything draining her energy. She installed Quicken® and automated all her bill paying, shared cooking with a friend so she only had to cook every other week, hired a college student to run weekly errands, hired a gardener to handle the yard and a twice-a-week housekeeper. Releasing these chores from her routine allowed her to feel more in control, focus more at work, have more quality family time and even have time for herself.

By using The Effective EDGE, Susan found she was better able to contribute at work and was more present with her patients. When she was at home, she was able to focus on her family and enjoy her time with them.

After several years of success at the hospital, she opened her own practice, focusing on reconstructive surgery for breast cancer patients. Today, she is energized and feels successful in all areas of her life.

Through the course of this book, you have learned a number of practical strategies and techniques you can use to be more productive and thrive ... beginning today.

You may implement them all now or integrate them, one by one, into your routine. Over time, these tools can help you be more proactive and strategic, ensure you are working on the right things, reduce and manage interruptions and have meaningful experiences outside of work.

It doesn't matter where you are. What matters is that you begin. Remember, it may feel like writing with the other hand at first, but soon you will be thriving.

Throughout this book, we've talked about qualities, practices and behaviors of the Thriving Professional. To summarize, Thriving Professionals:

- ♦ Possess a desire to thrive – no longer satisfied with surviving or just getting by.

- ♦ Use The Effective EDGE seamless system – they don't have to wonder where things are or when they promised something.

- ♦ Are no-brainers. They use their heads for creative problem solving, client work-arounds, strategic and outside-the-box thinking – not remembering To-Do's.

- ♦ Make fast, effective decisions that they trust – now and tomorrow.

- ♦ See the forest and the trees and are able to manage both. They plan projects quickly and succinctly and keep all of their projects in front of them.

- ♦ Take time to re-charge themselves weekly – to ensure they are executing on the right things.

- ♦ Keep their agreements in their systems – not in their heads!

- ♦ Minimize interruptions – from their own heads and others.

- ♦ Create powerful Intentions to create what they want.

- ♦ Organize, orchestrate and execute on everything that matters to them – not just work.

- ♦ Are focused, relaxed and confident.

♦ Have room to be creative, expressive and expansive in their approach to their lives.

I sometimes say that I was a graduate of the school of hard knocks. At most, I was the master of how to survive. There isn't much joy, expression, creativity or productivity in it. I realized that there was nothing great or powerful or life-giving about surviving. It was when I thrived that I let my own light shine – that it allowed others to do the same. I made the changes for me, but also for my son, my family, my employees, my clients and the lives of whomever I touched.

As we bring the written journey to a close and you start your personal journey to thrive, I want to share with you a piece of my favorite quote. Marianne Williamson wrote these words for Nelson Mandela. They are strong and powerful and they keep me inspired and moving toward thriving.

> *Our deepest fear is not that we are inadequate. Our deepest fear is that we are powerful beyond measure. It is our light, not our darkness that most frightens us. We ask ourselves, who am I to be brilliant, gorgeous, talented and fabulous? Actually, who are you not to be? You are a child of God. Your playing small in the world doesn't serve the world. There's nothing enlightened about shrinking so that other people won't feel insecure around you. You were born to manifest the Glory of God that is within us. It's not just in some of us; it's in everyone. And as we let our own light shine, we unconsciously give other people permission to do the same. As we are liberated from our own fear, our presence automatically liberates other.*
> – Marianne Williamson
> (excerpted from Nelson Mandela's inaugural address)

My hope is that you create the life that you want – the work life and all of your life – that you truly thrive!

So, as I asked in Chapter 1, *are you ready to thrive?*

NEXT STEPS: FIVE WAYS TO BRING THE EFFECTIVE EDGE MESSAGE TO YOUR ORGANIZATION.

1. **Keynote Presentations** – Topics to help professionals gain relaxed control over their busy lives and begin thriving. Lengths vary by audience. Christina Randle's business and organizational skills, coupled with her experience in personal and transformational development, add a motivational and inspirational quality to any program.

2. **Getting The EDGE™ Workshop** – Getting the EDGE™ is a nine-hour, instructor-led workshop for up to 20 people. Proven self-management topics are delivered on a fast-track basis, using your own inbox, files and tasks – leaving no application gap! You'll have The Effective EDGE, a feeling of relaxed control and focus returning to your office with a life-changing way of thinking!

3. **Getting The EDGE™ Online training program** – Online learning version of Getting The EDGE. Ideal for remote and seasonal employees.

4. **Getting It Together with Your PIM PDF® Booklet.** Quickly adapt The Effective EDGE to your PIM e-mail client using this instructive PowerPoint® Presentation. Available for MS Outlook, Novell GroupWise and Lotus Notes.

5. **The EDGE™ Laminate** – This handy reminder card provides two components of The Effective EDGE right at your fingertips. One side includes The EDGE Deciding Model™ while the other details The EDGE Weekly Recharge™.

www.**EffectiveEdge**.com 512.474.5200
e-mail: info@effectiveedge.com

About the Author

Christina Tibbits-Randle
The Effective Edge, Founder and CEO

Named Dallas' Most Organized Person by
D Magazine, Christina is a living testament that
her organizational methodologies work as well in
practice as on paper. Born in a small Texas town
to quite humble beginnings, she learned to battle adversity at a
young age. She tried college, and at 21, she was divorced with a
son, no degree and knew something had to change. She became
a student of productivity and life.

Now a skilled professional with Master's degrees in both psychology
and philosophy, Christina has been developing and delivering
productivity coaching and training programs for a variety of
clients including Dell, Intuit, PepsiCo, and numerous other
Fortune 500 companies. Her programs transform her clients'
efficiency, effectiveness and bottom-line results. Her experiences
and background add a motivational and inspirational quality to
The Effective Edge programs.

In her approach to her business and personal life she constantly
questions what helps people be their best, perform their best and
live their best life. Christina never waivers from the belief that it
really is possible to thrive, a way of life she bestows to all her clients.

Accelerate Personal Growth Resources

12 Choices…That Lead to Your Success is about success…how to achieve it, keep it and enjoy it…by making better choices. $14.95

Orchestrating Attitude translates the incomprehensible into the actionable. It cuts through the clutter to deliver inspiration and application so you can orchestrate your attitude…and your success. $9.95

Conquering Adversity – Six Strategies to Move You and Your Team Through Tough Times is a practical guide to help people and organizations deal with the unexpected and move forward through adversity. $14.95

107 Ways to Stick to It What's the REAL secret to success? Learn the secrets from the world's highest achievers. These 107 practical, inspiring tips will help you stick to it and WIN! $9.95

The Ant and the Elephant is a different kind of book for a different kind of leader! A great story that teaches that we must lead ourselves before we can expect to be an effective leader of others. $12.95

Too Many Emails contains dozens of tips and techniques to increase your email effectiveness and efficiency. $9.95

175 Ways to Get More Done in Less Time has 175 really good suggestions that will help you get things done faster…usually better. $9.95

Becoming the Obvious Choice is a roadmap showing each employee how they can maintain their motivation, develop their hidden talents, and become the best. $9.95

You and Your Network is profitable reading for those who want to learn how to develop healthy relationships with others. "I think every living person should read and re-read this book. It can change your life."
– David Cottrell $9.95

136 Effective Presentation Tips is a powerful handbook providing 136 practical, easy to use tips to make every presentation a success. $9.95

Silver Bullets contains straightforward tips on how to gain success while keeping your wits about you. $14.95

The NEW CornerStone Perpetual Calendar, a compelling collection of quotes about leadership and life, is perfect for office desks, school and home countertops. $14.95

CornerStone Collection of Note Cards Sampler Pack is designed to make it easy for you to show appreciation for your team, clients and friends. The awesome photography and your personal message written inside will create a lasting impact. Pack of 12 (one each of all 12 designs) $24.95

Visit www.**CornerStoneLeadership**.com for additional books and resources.

YES! Please send me extra copies of *Getting It Together!*
1-30 copies $14.95   31-100 copies $13.95   101+ copies $12.95

| *Getting It Together* | _____ copies X _____ | = $ _____ |

Additional Personal Growth Resources

Accelerate Personal Growth Package   _____ pack(s) X $139.95   = $ _____
(Includes one each of all items listed
   on page 118.)

Other Books

_____	_____ copies X _____	= $ _____
_____	_____ copies X _____	= $ _____
_____	_____ copies X _____	= $ _____
_____	_____ copies X _____	= $ _____
_____	_____ copies X _____	= $ _____

Shipping & Handling $ _____

Subtotal $ _____

Sales Tax (8.25%-TX Only) $ _____

Total (U.S. Dollars Only) $ _____

Shipping and Handling Charges

Total $ Amount	Up to $49	$50-$99	$100-$249	$250-$1199	$1200-$2999	$3000+
Charge	$6	$9	$16	$30	$80	$125

Name _____ Job Title _____

Organization _____ Phone_____

Shipping Address _____ Fax _____

Billing Address _____E-mail _____
(required when ordering PowerPoint® Presentation)

City _____ State _____ ZIP_____

❏ Please invoice (Orders over $200) Purchase Order Number (if applicable) _____

Charge Your Order: ❏ MasterCard   ❏ Visa   ❏ American Express

Credit Card Number _____ Exp. Date _____

Signature _____

❏ Check Enclosed (Payable to: CornerStone Leadership)

Fax	**Mail**	**Phone**
972.274.2884	**P.O. Box 764087**	**888.789.5323**
	Dallas, TX 75376	

www.**CornerStoneLeadership**.com

Thank you for reading *Getting It Together*.
We hope it has assisted you in your quest for
personal and professional growth.

CornerStone Leadership is committed to provide new
and enlightening products to organizations worldwide.
Our mission is to fuel knowledge with practical resources
that will accelerate your team's productivity,
success and job satisfaction!

Best wishes for your continued success.

CornerStone
Leadership Institute
www.CornerStoneLeadership.com

Start a crusade in your organization —
have the courage to learn, the vision to lead,
and the passion to share.